DISCARDED

WHITE AND BLACK
UNDER THE OLD REGIME

Victoria V. Clayton.

WHITE AND BLACK
UNDER THE OLD REGIME

..BY..
VICTORIA V. CLAYTON

WITH INTRODUCTION BY
FREDERIC COOK MOREHOUSE

BOOKS FOR LIBRARIES PRESS
FREEPORT, NEW YORK

First Published 1899
Reprinted 1970

STANDARD BOOK NUMBER:
8369-5371-1

LIBRARY OF CONGRESS CATALOG CARD NUMBER:
70-119928

PRINTED IN THE UNITED STATES OF AMERICA

TABLE OF CONTENTS.

Introduction.		5
Author's Preface.		13
I.	Parentage and History of Early Days.	17
II.	Other Events of Childhood—School Days—Close of School Life.	28
III.	Return Home.	38
IV.	The Kansas Episode — Seeing the Country.	62
V.	Return to Alabama — Home Incidents — Mutterings of War—Incidents at Pensacola. — Extempore Manufacturing.	82
VI.	Home Trials and Labors — Cloth Making — Various Illustrative Incidents.	113
VII.	Close of the War—Incidents of Reconstruction — Extract from Judge Clayton's Charge to the Grand Jury — Beginning Life Over.	150
VIII.	Becoming a Slaveholder Again—Last Days of General Clayton.	184

ILLUSTRATIONS.

FULL PAGE HALF TONES.

The Authoress.	FRONTISPIECE.
The Authoress in Younger Days.	16-17
Stephen Elliott, D.D., Bishop of Georgia, 1841-1866.	34-35
The Old Homestead, Clayton, Ala.	46-47
General Clayton, in the Kansas War.	62-63
Brig. Gen. Grierson, U. S. A.	148-149
General Clayton, Judge.	156-157
President's Mansion, University of Alabama.	190-191

OTHER ILLUSTRATIONS.

Group of Negro Children.	22
"Say yer Pra'rs, Chile."	39
Carding and Weaving.	114
Bishop Quintard.	138
"Uncle Joe."	168
Bishop Cobbs.	189
Bishop Wilmer.	189

INTRODUCTION.

THE civilized world never again will see a people who are called happy because they have no history. There was a time—it may be said to have terminated with the reign of Henry VII. in England—when History was a record of kings and knights, of wars of conquest and quarrels about succession to thrones. We have begun to be civilized since those days; and in a few centuries more we shall no doubt be able to write, "Happy is that people who have a long history." For History now-a-days is the record of the development, the advances, the progress of a people.

That is why a sketch such as these

covers enfold, is worthy of a place in a historical collection. The modesty of the authoress, which, according to a Gælic proverb, is "the beauty of women," and according to Diogenes, is "the color of virtue," leads her to underrate the value of her own work. Her noble husband, at whose request, before his death, these pages were written, was one of the most eminent men in the South during and after the great conflict. He is said to have been the first man in Alabama to enlist in the war for the Confederacy. As Major General in the Confederate army, Judge of the circuit court of Alabama, and President of the University of Alabama, he may easily be picked out as a true representative of the men of the Old South; as his white-haired widow, whose sweet nobility of character shines out in her every deed, is of the women of the same.

And the Claytons have been no unknown quantity in the history of the nation. The senior branch, whose ancestor, Joshua Clayton, came over with William Penn, and settled in Delaware, has given to the country three United States Senators, one of them being also the Secretary of State under President Taylor, who negotiated for the United States and gave his name to, the Clayton-Bulwer treaty. The junior branch of the family, which is settled in Virginia and Georgia, traces its history to John Clayton, attorney general of colonial Virginia, and has also produced the renowned botanist, son of the attorney general, a senator from Georgia, and a number of men familiar in the local history of Virginia.

It is the middle line, the descendants of James Clayton, who settled in Maryland at about the dawn of the eighteenth century, of which Major General Henry D. Clayton, the husband of this present authoress, may be said to be the most prominent figure. These Claytons were more roving, and have planted branches of their line in Maryland, in North Carolina, in Alabama, in New York, and in California. One fair daughter of the race came to Wisconsin to make a home for him who writes this introduction, and to transplant in the hardy North, those same noble virtues which have made the name renowned throughout the South. Two of the sons of General and Mrs. Clayton are at this present time Members of Congress, the one from Alabama and the other from New York. A brother, a Captain in the Confederate army, was fatally wounded at Murfreesboro.

For myself, a son of the North, trained in the very opposite political principles for which the Claytons and the South have contended, it is a great happiness to introduce this simple memoir, which, in its way, is an *Apologia* for the Old South. The South has given to me the dearest treasure a man may seek; and in return for it I give the South a true, warm affection, seeing the nobility which has lain back of her history, appreciating her problems, past and present, which one can only fully know when he really knows her people, sympathizing with her in troubles which would have driven into anarchy a less noble race, condoning her very faults and mistakes.

For all human progress has moved along in a blundering sort of fashion, and we have stumbled into more promised lands than we ever set out to conquer. I can see God in History—the Holy Ghost brooding over many a Chaos since first the history of Creation was written. He truly has moved "in a mysterious way," and has used our very blundering and stumbling, "His wonders to perform."

I wish the younger generation would try to know the South, as I have learned to know it. The Spanish war has shown to the world, what we Americans have long known, that we are again a united country. But we do not understand each other's problems as we ought to, and in our political relations, we are content to put on our war paint, and flourish our tomahawks, and pretend that the integrity of the Constitution, if not of the whole human race, depends on our scalping a few windmills that politicians have laboriously pushed into our way. And all the while we have lucid intervals in which we see that it is all a great ghost dance, and that they are the ghosts and goblins of dead issues and dead warriors that are keeping alive the bonfire in the camp. And if in spite of all the ghosts, the flames of past discords will burn low, the politicians will gather by the clans and discuss what new "issues" they can devise, to keep the windmills in the road and the people apart.

And that they term Politics.

But some day we shall learn better. And these quiet annals, such as this which I now introduce to a people who truly intend to do right, as the American people intend to do, will help to speed the day.

May God do the rest!

FREDERIC C. MOREHOUSE.

Milwaukee, August, 1899.

We live in deeds, not years; in thoughts, not breaths;
In feelings, not in figures on a dial.
    He most lives
Who thinks most, feels the noblest, acts the best.

PREFACE.

THE writer of this biography is a woman now over sixty years of age. Her life has been spent entirely in the South, and covers the most eventful and stirring period of the Nation's history. She is able to recall the happy days of Southern prosperity prior to the civil war. She knows experimentally and by observation what slavery was. She realizes its happiness and sorrow; she has felt the anxiety and experienced the sacrifices incident to the struggle; she has sustained the bitter loss which the defeat of the South finally entailed.

She lays this humble and unpretentious biography before the public for the following reasons:

First, it was her husband's request, made shortly before his death, that she should make record in this way of her experiences, and she feels that his wishes in the matter should be respected. And, therefore, though utterly unaccustomed to literary effort, she tries to fulfil his desire.

Again, she thinks her simple story may not be entirely without fruit in giving her Northern readers a more just conception of what the system of Southern slavery actually was, as it existed in many, if not in most, instances. She thinks the time has come in her life when she can recount her experiences and tell her tale without a suggestion of bitterness, being only concerned to present things as they were, and to declare her convictions as they existed.

And, finally, she trusts that the story

of her life will be of interest to her children and grandchildren, as well as to family connections and friends.

1899.   V. V. C.

Mrs. Clayton.

WHITE AND BLACK UNDER THE OLD REGIME.

I.

PARENTAGE AND HISTORY OF EARLY DAYS.

> "O Reader! had you in your mind
>   Such stories as silent thought can bring,
> O gentle Reader! you would find
>   A tale in everything.
> What more I have to say is short,
>   And you must kindly take it:
> It is no tale; but, should you think,
>   Perhaps a tale you'll make it."
> —*Wordsworth.*

MY father, John Linguard Hunter, was of English and Scottish descent, his ancestors belonging to the

Gentry.* He was a planter by profession, owning at one time two large plantations in the State of South Carolina.

In 1835, hearing many marvellous stories of the great productiveness of the land in the State of Alabama, he was induced to sell his plantations in his old native State and move to Alabama. Here he found everything in a crude, unsettled condition. I was only two years old, and consequently know nothing of the country at that time except from hearing the older members of the family tell about it.

The little town selected for our home was merely an Indian village then. Many tribes of these natives roved over the country. Oftentimes they were very troublesome, and finally became so hostile to the white settlers that they were obliged, in self-defense, to resort

---

*He married when quite young, Sarah Elizabeth Bowler, who was of English parentage. She was my mother.

Parentage and History of Early Days.

to some means of driving them out. This meant war, which began in February, 1836.

My father and oldest brother joined the army formed for the purpose of making the red man take up his march towards the setting sun. My mother and her children were sent up into middle Georgia to remain while these hostilities, called the Indian War, lasted.

When peace was restored and it was safe for us to return, we came back to our home in Irwinton, now Eufaula. A house for our occupation had been almost finished in the village before our flight, and my mother found on our return that the soldiers had used it as a barracks, and in consequence it was injured to some extent. She cared not, though, for this; she was so thankful to be free from savage faces peeping and prying around the premises. She had been very much afraid of these savages, and when the squaws visited her she used to give them anything they asked for; and in this way we were often deprived of a favorite dress or of other things which we prized greatly. Being fond of gay colors, they were always sure to want the red dresses, and, to our discomfort, carried them off.

Speaking of the productiveness of the soil, brings to my mind what I have heard of the vast quantity of strawberries that covered the earth in the spring. The Indians would gather them to sell to the white settlers; picking them from native vines that had never received any cultivation except the burning off of the forest once a year.

Upon his return to Irwinton, my father began to put his home in order, arranging for the white family in the village, and for the most part of the colored families on the plantation. The plantation lay on the banks of the Chattahoochie River, about two miles from the village. Here the greater number of his slaves lived. My father was a slave-holder by inheritance, never having known anything else. "Our thoughts, our morals, our most fixed beliefs, are consequences of our place of birth."

When fond memory carries me back to my childhood's happy days, these colored friends on the old plantation occupy a very important place. I recall the commodious carriage, the bay horses, and old Uncle Abram seated on the driver's seat to take us, the children, through the beautiful woods, to make a visit to the old "maumers" down on the plantation. Our mother taught us to respect age in whatever position we found it, and we always called the older women "maumers" as marks of respect due their years. How dear these scenes are to us even now!

"Pictured in memory's mellowing glass how sweet
Our infant days, our infant joys to greet;
To roam in fancy in each cherished scene,
The village churchyard, and the village green,
The woodland walk remote, the green wood glade,
The mossy seat beneath the hawthorn's shade,
The whitewashed cottage where the woodbine grew,
And the favorite haunts our childhood knew:
These long lost scenes to me the past restore,
Each humble friend, each pleasure now no more."—*Kirke White.*

Every slave family possessed a garden, truck patch, chicken house and a lot of hens, and, from these sources, always had something nice to present to us, their young "misses." We cherished these humble presents, peanuts, fresh eggs, and the like, as though they were of intrinsic value. Their little cottages were arranged so as to form streets. After making the round of visits, not slighting any, but going in to see every one at home, sitting and chatting with all, we usually finished our calls at Uncle Sam's house. He was the foreman on the plantation, and had a more pretentious home. His wife, maum Flora, would entertain us most royally with bread and milk under the grand old oaks that sheltered the space around the door. These two humble friends would express much sincere delight at our accepting their generous hospitality. I have spent many happy hours with these good people in the long ago. The old man was a Methodist preacher, and close by his house stood a neat little building, in which he gathered all the children on Sunday morning to teach them their duty to God and man. Later in the day the adults assembled for worship. Frequently a visiting preacher would assist Uncle Sam in ministering to these people on a Sunday. The old man could read the Bible, but his education did not extend much beyond that and weighing the cotton as it was gathered from the fields, and putting down the weights for my father's inspection. Uncle Sam was, I believe, a good Christian man, and these people looked up to him with almost reverence.

My father was a kind, indulgent master, and I think I have never in the world met with happier people than were these simple uneducated blacks.

At our home in town were several slave families besides the house servants. One large, old woman I remember so well—maum Eva. She served as monthly nurse to the ladies over the town, and would pay my mother so much each month; "Hiring her time," she termed it. In this way she made considerable money and lived well, always having something nice to eat in her house. I thought she made the most marvellous "marvels" and honey cakes I ever tasted. Occasionally she invited the children of her white folks (as she called us) to take tea with her, and those teas were always enjoyed to the fullest extent by us.

Maum Kate, the washwoman, also deserves mention. She lived over on the hill near the banks of the Chattahoochie River, where we could watch the boats ascending and descending the beautiful river. She always had a loaf of nice bread awaiting our coming.

We dearly loved these old friends and thought their food the best in the world.

The hog-killing times were always glorious to us children. In those days we had no railroads, and transportation through the country was carried on by private means. The meat raised for exportation in Kentucky and Tennessee was not cured in those states and sent off as now, but the porkers were driven in great herds into other states and sold on their feet, and thus the farmers bought their meat and cured it themselves for the plantations. Hog-killing for home use was a big time; especially to the negroes, who enjoyed the back bones and spare ribs hugely. I can, in imagination, see them now with their thick, greasy lips and laughing eyes. Everything was conducted in primitive style. There were no sausage stuffers and cutters like those of to-day, but one large room was filled with blocks sawed from forest trees, and at each block sat a woman, adorned with white apron and head-kerchief, chopping with a hatchet the sausage meat—chop, chop—then turn over and chop again until the meat was ready to be cased. Then the frying pan was in demand as the seasoning went on, to ascertain when palatable. Then the stuffing began, with no machine but a piece of white oak splint. Twisted round and round over this, the case was drawn and the meat pushed in and pulled down with the fingers. Thus sausages were made on the old Southern plantations. We would stand around and watch these operations with child-like pleasure. My mother always had a goodly supply of good sausage on hand for the winter.

II.

OTHER EVENTS OF CHILDHOOD—SCHOOL DAYS—CLOSE OF SCHOOL LIFE.

AN old aunt of my mother had come to make her home with us. She was a peculiar woman and a devotedly zealous Methodist. She built the first Methodist church in Barbour County. It is now standing in Eufaula, but is used as a Hebrew Synagogue, the Methodists having sold it and built other churches. Many a day have I spent, when about eight years old, going round calling with Aunt Polly, as everybody called her. She was a Mrs. Barefield, but few knew her except as

Aunt Polly. She never left home without her sack, which she wore suspended from her waist, containing a bottle of cologne, one of paragoric, one of liquid assafœtida, and a silver teaspoon. All these were fitted in their respective places, and this strange contrivance was concealed by her over-dress. She also carried an umbrella and fan. Thus she was always ready for heat, cold or sunshine, sickness or health. These conveniences were oftentimes brought into requisition in her visits to the families of the town. With this dear old aunt I began my first church work.

In the spring of 1843 this aunt was taken to Paradise. Very soon after, our darling mother followed, and our happy family was broken up. The older children had married and gone, but there were four of us left. My father sent the two older girls to a boarding school, carried on by Mrs. Caroline Lee Hense, so my youngest sister and I were left with father in our sad old home. The servants were as good to us as they could be, but Father's business necessitated his absence a considerable portion of the time; consequently he determined it best for us to go and live with our married sisters. I spent several years very happily in my sister Violetta's family, although I never could speak of my sainted mother without shedding tears.

Our once rustic little village had by this time grown to be quite a town, and supported good schools. My brother, with whom I was now staying, had a friend living some miles in the country, who had a daughter he wished to send in town to attend school. She came to stay with us, and shared my room. We became good friends, and after her sojourn with us for several months, her father came to take her home for a few days, and invited me to accompany her to their country home, some fifteen miles distant, which I was delighted to do. When we reached Abbie's home, the news of a marriage near by greeted us, and the next day we attended this real country wedding, and strangely primitive and uncouth it was to me! The following day I was still more excited by the novelty of events. The entire neighborhood was invited to what they called an "infair" at my friend's house. In society we would term it a reception, but these country people called it an infair. Early in the morning the crowd began to gather from the surrounding country for many miles and no sooner had they assembled than dancing began; not the fashionable round dances of to-day, but the old Cotillion and Virginia Reel. I, being a city young lady only about twelve years old, but considering myself much older, was quite the belle of the occasion, and entered into the rural sports with all the gusto of youth. When I think of it now I am reminded of Goldsmith's *Deserted Village:*

"Where humble happiness endeared each scene;
* * * * * * * * * * *
His best companions, innocence and health,
And his best riches, ignorance of wealth."

Among this large company of simple, unsophisticated men, there was one somewhat above the others in honors, as he was Justice of the Peace, and often in his little rustic office sat in judgment on the breakers of the law. His name was Young Wood. He was Abbie's uncle, and every one in the neighborhood called him Uncle Young. He particularly admired me, and would say, "She is a pretty little gal." He was an odd-looking old man. I once heard a boy say, "Why, Uncle Young looks like a big apple with two straws stuck in it."

He was as good and true a citizen as Barbour County could boast. The old man was a great politician, and in after years he became a strong friend of my husband. I never saw the old man again until after I had married and become the mother of several children, and then he came to our home. I was in the garden gathering berries for tea, when my husband came out and said to me:

"Victoria, Uncle Young has come to see us."

I followed him into the house immediately and greeted this kind old friend cordially. He seemed disappointed in not meeting the rosy young girl he had admired so extravagantly, but a staid woman instead. He scanned me very closely and, turning to my husband, whom he always called Henry, he said:

"Henry, she was the prettiest little thing I ever saw the day she was at the 'infair' at Jim's."

I said, "Well, Uncle Young, I lack

considerable of being the pretty little girl now."

Whereupon he replied, "I'll be d—d if you don't."

This would have seemed exceedingly ill-bred and uncouth in any one else; not so, though, with this humble, good-meaning man. We enjoyed a hearty laugh at his strongly expressed disappointment.

To take up again the thread of my narrative: I remained in my sister's family until my fifteenth year, when my father, who was an Episcopalian, took me to the school of Bishop Stephen Elliott. The Bishop at that time had the supervision of Christ College, a female institute belonging to the Diocese of Georgia, situated at Montpelier, about fourteen miles from Macon. There I remained two years and learned to love God's Holy Church. This love has grown day by day in all these succeed-

Stephen Elliott, D. D.,
Bishop of Georgia, 1841-1866.

ing years. The school generally numbered about one hundred girls from our best families, and they were all devoted to the dear Bishop and lovely Mrs. Elliott.

Many of our teachers were from the North, and were very intellectual and highly cultivated ladies, and I was much attached to several of them. Some of my happiest days were spent here at Montpelier, and memory still retains some lovely pictures of our life in these classic halls. The school was conducted somewhat unlike most boarding schools. It was divided into sections, each section consisting of about twelve girls. One teacher had special charge of a section. She was expected to look after the girls under her care with regard to their welfare in every way. Each teacher had a parlor, called her section room, where all of her girls were obliged to assemble at the ringing of the bell, very soon after the evening meal. Here the girls were required to bring some sewing, fancy work, or plain sewing, as each wished, and, while we were learning the use of the needle, one of the girls would read aloud. In this way the section room became an important feature in the education of the girls. Here we read Milton's *Paradise Lost,* and many other standard works.

I shall ever remember the day Bishop Elliott became forty-one years old. We all knew when his birthday was. For several weeks beforehand we were making preparations for the surprise and happiness of this "man of God." When he awoke in the morning, the first thing that greeted him was a beautiful pair of chamber slippers with a dainty note of love from the section composed of the smaller girls; then in the sitting-room there awaited him a token of love from each teacher and her girls. When he entered the breakfast room, the table was all wreathed in flowers. The Bishop then made us a little speech, expressing his appreciation, and school duties were suspended for the day. How happy we all were!

III.

RETURN HOME.

AFTER two years' stay at boarding school, I returned to the old homestead and found my father all alone except the faithful family slaves. In those days, with the better class of citizens, such servants were numerous, and each had his special charge. In our household there were Middleton, who waited on my father and kept the dining room in order; the cook, maum Louisa; the washwoman, maum Kate; and Uncle Abram, the man-servant who cared for the horses. There were all these servants with so little to occupy them; yet they were cared for as members of the family, fed and clothed, and attended by the family doctor when sick. They were not taken on social equality with their owners, any more than the servants at the North would be. My father's slaves all looked up to him with loving respect. On my return home, a girl of

"SAY YER PRA'RS, CHILE."

twelve summers was brought in from the plantation for my special service.

I recall a sad incident of this period of my life. On the death of my mother,

her estate, which consisted of slaves, was divided among the children. In the number that came to my inheritance was a bright, intelligent boy. He acted as errand boy about the premises and was very useful. One day he asked permission to go with another boy of nearly the same age to gather blackberries. After some importunity on his part I consented to let him go. The two happy boys ran off in glee, promising to be good boys. It was the last time that Daniel was ever seen. His comrade returned in great excitement to say that Daniel was drowned in the river. We had a search made and the shore watched, but never could find his body. This incident was a great sorrow to my young heart, for I had become much attached to him, as he was good and affectionate.

My two sisters, older than myself, who were sent to boarding school after our mother's death, had married at the early age of sixteen, and had households of their own. In those days our Southern girls married very young. The reason of this was, I suppose, that there were so many more young men in the South than young women, that the girls were in demand. A large number of young men came from the North to engage in business here. On attending church I have often looked over the congregation and seen many more young gentlemen than ladies present. Now it is quite the reverse. We often see a congregation composed almost entirely of ladies.

In our dear old home I found the management of domestic duties in the hands of the negroes. I at once proceeded to take the supervision of the household into my own hands, not only the little every-day matters about the house, but also the weighing-out and providing supplies to be sent down to the plantation. All these things had been entrusted to the negroes by my father. They had gotten along pretty well; still, I thought I could improve on the existing management, and accordingly went to work in earnest.

I staid closely at home attending to these duties. I did not know that any one in town was taking note of my conduct. But by some means, it soon became the talk of the town that the young lady just returned from college was making herself a practicable business woman. A young man recently graduated with the highest honors from a college in Virginia, came to Eufaula for the purpose of studying law, and hearing of her, he remarked, "Must seek her acquaintance; she will make a good wife." No practical man worth the favorable consideration of a young lady, desires a useless woman to share with him the "changes and chances of this mortal life." This young man studied law, was admitted to the bar, and soon procured the position of assistant in the Circuit Clerk's office at Clayton, the county seat. He bought a home there and finally asked me to share it with him.

Marriage, in my judgment, was too serious a thing to enter into without careful consideration; therefore I asked for time to dwell on the proposition. He returned to his duties at Clayton, and some weeks thereafter I concluded to visit a sister living some miles from Clayton. After spending a week there, on Saturday afternoon, looking down the road, we beheld my friend, Mr. Clayton, approaching through a dreadful rain storm. It had been raining all the afternoon, but notwithstanding rain and storm, love stimulated him to encounter all difficulties, however great, to hear the decision. Next morning one of the neighbors came over to visit the family and finding Mr. Clayton present, he expressed much astonishment, saying:

"When did you come out, Mr. Clayton?"

He replied, "Yesterday afternoon."

Whereupon this neighbor said:

"The weather was very inclement, very inclement indeed."

This remark and his suspicious manner were very funny to us who had decided to travel life's path together.

This was in September, and on the ninth day of January thereafter, in the year 1850, we were married at my father's house in Eufaula. I was in my eighteenth year and Mr. Clayton in his twenty-second, a youthful couple, happy and joyous, full of hope for the long future that lay before us.

He took me to a dear little home in

Clayton where we began house-keeping, with three servants: my cook, Harriet, inherited from my mother's estate; a boy, Ned, given my husband by his father; and little Annie, Harriet's daughter.

Attached to our home was a field, and Ned cultivated that in addition to the duties about the yard. We kept a horse and buggy and in this way could have the land cultivated, and use the horse for pleasure driving, too. We made food for our horse and cow, and secured many little luxuries for ourselves, none of which we enjoyed more than the sugar-cane as we sat by the cheerful hearth during the long winter evenings. I found little Annie not only useful in saving me steps, but a real comfort when I was left alone. I soon became very much attached to her and she was like my shadow, following me everywhere.

Mr. Clayton applied himself closely to his business, and, as every lawyer knows, had a great deal of writing to do; more than is often required now, because then there was more money in circulation and consequently more litigation. He would bring his books home at night, and after tea I would call for him as he would write, thus enabling him to finish his allotted task very soon. Then we would spend some time reading Shakespeare and other standard writers.

Here in this little cottage we spent many happy days, and here it was I experienced the joy of becoming a mother.

"For all unfinish'd was Love's jeweled ring,
Till set with this soft pearl;
How pure, how perfect seem'd the gift to me."

One of the loveliest pictures in nature is a young mother with her first born. And nothing develops the good in

The Old Clayton Homestead.

At Clayton, Ala.

woman like becoming a mother; her whole heart goes out in charity to the world.

We lived in this house two years, when my husband having saved up enough money, purchased a farm near by, and we came into the inheritance of more slaves. We sold our dear little first home and moved to the farm. It was only one mile from the court house, and my husband would walk to and from his place of business. We gathered together our slaves and began a new life. Rules were made and everything was organized with reference to the comfort of all and profit to ourselves.

We had only eight grown negroes. One woman did the cooking for the whole household and the washing for the white family. I, with the help of my little girl, Annie, discharged the other duties of the house. The negroes were all called up early in the morning and went to the field before breakfast. The breakfast was prepared and sent to them. Their breakfast generally consisted of meat, ordinarily bacon, sometimes beef, hot coffee, and bread. At twelve o'clock they all returned to the house to feed the mules, eat their midday meal, and rest. The dinner consisted of meat, vegetables of different kinds, and bread, often fruit pies, especially in the summer season, and old fashioned pot pies cooked in a big oven. Apples baked with honey was a great dish for all at our house. After two hours' rest, the slaves returned to the field and remained until the setting sun warned them of the near approach of night. The evening meal was generally lighter than the others, milk taking the place of meat. Many of our farmers weighed out the rations weekly to their hands, letting them prepare their own meals; but my husband adopted his father's way of doing: having their meals cooked for them, so that the time allotted for rest could be spent literally at rest.

My reason for giving our usual bill of fare for our slaves is the many erroneous ideas on this subject. I recall an instance. A book agent from one of the Eastern States called one day to see if we would take one of his books. He was invited in and treated very politely. After an hour's conversation about the negro in the South, he asked if we fed them on cotton seed. We called in an old colored woman, who, when a slave, was the property of my father-in-law. She, after freedom, went to live with one of her grandchildren near Opelika, and Mr. Clayton hearing, while holding court in Opelika, that her children were unkind to her, had brought her to our home and we were taking care of her in her old age. Aunt Rose answered his numerous questions and amused us all very much.

In my home management I always tried to have an abundance of food for the entire family, but never forgot the injunction of our Lord after He had fed the five thousand persons. He said, "Gather up the fragments, that nothing be lost." I was brought up to believe that economy should be practised in all things as a Christan duty, and if one have more than one needs it should be divided with those who have not. "The poor ye have always with you." Thinking that the women would enjoy cooking a meal occasionally for their families, the custom adopted was that they should come on Saturday with their vessels to receive flour, sugar, lard, and other necessaries, besides the daily rations given them to cook. Each woman was provided with cooking utensils in her own home and was permitted to prepare food when not engaged in the regular labor for the day. Often on Sunday morning we have passed their doors and seen families gathered around tables on which very tempting breakfasts were spread. The women were all taught to cook plain food. They particularly excelled in making good beaten biscuits and plain corn bread.

By and by the family became large, both through natural increase of the negroes, and because my husband, at the close of each year, having saved up money enough to invest in something to increase our income, was naturally disposed to invest in slaves as being then the most available and profitable property in our section of the country.

We never raised the question for one moment as to whether slavery was right. We had inherited the institution from devout Christian parents. Slaves were held by pious relatives and friends and clergymen to whom we were accustomed to look up. The system of slave-holding was incorporated into our laws, and was regulated and protected by them. We read our Bible and accepted its teachings as the true guide in faith and morals. We understood literally our Lord's instructions to His chosen people, and applied them to our circumstances and surroundings. "Both thy bond-men, and thy bond-maids, which thou shalt have, shall be of the heathen that are round about you; of them shall ye buy bond-men and bond-maids. Moreover, of the children of the strangers that sojourn among you, of them shall ye buy and of their families that are with you, which they begot in your land; and they shall be your possession. And ye shall take them as an inheritance for your children after you, to inherit them for a possession; they shall be your bond-men forever; but over your brethren the children of Israel, ye shall not rule one over another with rigour" (Levit. xxiv. 44).

We understood how an angel of the Lord recognized the right of Sarai, Abram's wife, to the services of her slave, Hagar, and when she was running away, sent her back to her mistress.

"And the angel of the Lord found her by a fountain of water in the wilderness, by the fountain in the way to Shur.

"And he said, Hagar, Sarai's maid, whence comest thou? and whither wilt thou go? And she said, I flee from the face of my mistress Sarai.

"And the angel of the Lord said unto her, Return to thy mistress, and submit thyself under her hands" (Gen. xvi. 7-9).

We noticed also how, under the

Christian Dispensation, St. Paul did the same thing in a similar case:

"Hearing of thy love and faith which thou hast toward the Lord Jesus, and toward all saints;

"That the communication of thy faith may become effectual by the acknowledging of every good thing which is in you in Christ Jesus.

"For we have great joy and consolation in thy love, because the bowels of the saints are refreshed by thee, brother.

"Wherefore, though I might be much bold in Christ to enjoin thee that which is convenient,

"Yet for love's sake I rather beseech thee, being such an one as Paul the aged, and now also a prisoner of Jesus Christ.

"I beseech thee for my son Onesimus, whom I have begotten in my bonds:

"Which in time past was to thee unprofitable, but now profitable to thee and to me:

"Whom I have sent again: thou therefore receive him, that is mine own bowels" (Philemon 5-12).

And how the same apostle declared the mind of Christ upon the duties of slaves:

"Let as many servants as are under the yoke count their own masters worthy of all honour, that the name of God and His doctrine be not blasphemed.

"And they that have believing masters, let them not despise them, because they are brethren; but rather do them service, because they are faithful and beloved, partakers of the benefit.

"These things teach and exhort.

"If any man teach otherwise, and consent not to wholesome words, even the words of our Lord Jesus Christ, and to the doctrine which is according to godliness,

"He is proud, knowing nothing, but doting about questions and strifes of words, whereof cometh envy, strife, railings, evil surmisings,

"Perverse disputings of men of corrupt minds, and destitute of the truth, supposing that gain is godliness: from such withdraw thyself" (I. Tim. vi. 1-5).

And how he instructed St. Titus to exhort slaves to be obedient to their masters and to serve them faithfully:

"Exhort servants to be obedient unto their own masters, and to please them well in all things; not answering again;

"Not purloining, but showing all good fidelity; that they may adorn the doctrine of God our Saviour in all things" (Titus xi. 9, 10).

And how St. Peter gave the same instructions to Christian slaves:

"Servants, be subject to your masters with all fear; not only to the good and gentle, but also to the forward" (I. Peter xi. 18).

We simply and naturally understood that our slaves must be treated kindly and cared for spiritually, and so they were. We felt that we were responsible to God for our entire household.

I found it necessary to keep two cooks now instead of one, as heretofore. Every morning I would take my key basket on my arm and make the rounds, giving out to each cook the various articles of food to be cooked for both white and colored families for the ensuing day. I gave the preparation of the food my careful attention. And their clothes were comfortable, each garment cut out with my own hands.

In these days of plenty there was a meat house filled with good home-cured meat, a cellar filled with sugar, syrup,

ON INSPECTION SUNDAY MORNING.

wine, vinegar, and soap, a potato house filled with sweet potatoes, and also a store room containing the breadstuffs, and so forth.

We regarded slavery in a patriarchal sense. We were all one family, and, as master and mistress, heads of this family, we were responsible to the God we worshipped for these creatures to a very great extent, and we felt our responsibility, and cared for their bodies.

As to their religious training, every Sunday morning the mothers brought their little ones up to see me. Then I could satisfy myself as to the care they gave them, whether they had received a bath and suitable clothing for the holy day. Later the larger children presented themselves to be taught the Catechism. I used the little *Calvary Catechism,* prepared by Mrs. D. C. Weston. The adults were permitted to attend the different churches in town as they pleased, but when the sun hid himself behind the western hills, all were compelled to return home to feed and care for the horses, cows, etc. When the evening meal was over my dining room was in readiness for the reception of all the grown members of the family. They gathered there and took their respective seats. They were taught the Creed of the Holy Apostolic Church, the Lord's Prayer, and the Ten Commandments; that is, all who could be taught, for some of them never could learn to repeat them, but understood the meaning sufficiently to lead a right life.

Sometimes I would read a short sermon to them. They sang hymns, and we closed with prayer to our Heavenly Father.

> "Glorious is the blending
> Of right affections, climbing or descending
> Along a scale of light and life with cares
> Alternate."

Just at this time we were visited by a great sorrow. The dread angel of death entered our happy, peaceful home and bore away our dear first-born son. We tried to submit, and to say as Job did in his affliction: "What! Shall we receive good at the hands of God, and shall we not receive evil?"

> "There is no flock however watched and tended
>   But one dead lamb is there.
> There is no fireside howsoe'er defended
>   But has one vacant chair."—*Longfellow.*

Here we lived in this quiet country home for some years, my husband going in to his business every morning, and I always busy at home caring for our family, both white and black. Every little negro on the place would come to me if he thought he received injustice at the hands of any one. These little negroes would hunt the hens' nests and bring me the eggs, and receive one or more eggs for their trouble and honesty. They were always happy in their innocent childhood. And these same negroes now, after all the changes, whenever I meet them, express their love for me in every possible way.

In 1855 all of our children had whooping cough, and my third child, a sweet babe of eight months, and also a colored child of the same age, were taken from us.

IV.

THE KANSAS EPISODE—SEEING THE COUNTRY.

THIS brings us to 1856, when Kansas Territory was seeking admission into the Union as a state. All the Southern people were interested in having it admitted as a slave state, consequently were desirous of sending out emigrants to settle there. A considerable amount of money was contributed for the purpose by the States of Alabama and Georgia. This money was entrusted to my husband for the purpose of taking out a body of emigrants and settling them in the Territory so as to secure their votes for the South in the coming election.

General H. D. Clayton,
In the Kansas War.

The Kansas Episode. 63

On the first day of August he was ready to leave, and wishing me to accompany him, our children were left with their grandmother. My husband's brother was living with us, and we knew that our faithful old black Joe, and his wife, Nancy, now my cook, would do all they could to have things progress satisfactorily on the plantation during our absence. Thus we left our home, our interests, to do what we thought a good for our country. How differently we would have acted had we possessed the eye of prophecy to look into the eventful future that lay before us! But it is, I think, a kind and merciful Providence which hides the future from us. "Sufficient unto the day is the evil thereof."

We left Eufaula, Alabama, early in August, gathering emigrants at every station as we journeyed through the two states. Finally they were all gathered under Mr. Clayton as leader, and they numbered about one hundred. We traveled by rail until we reached Nashville, Tenn. There a boat was chartered and we all took passage down the Cumberland. The river was very low and full of shoals at all times, and particularly so at this time, consequently we experienced a tedious time getting on in our journey. Sometimes the boat would be fast bound on a bar in the river and the crew would tie a large rope to a tree on shore, and by means of a windlass in front and the men lifting at the same time, they would succeed in moving forward.

Finally, after much patient waiting, we reached Cairo, where the Cumberland empties into the Great Father of Waters. Here our tents were spread on the banks of the river, and I, for the first time in my life, slept under so light a covering from the dews as a tent. I cared not for this.

> "Hope, like the glimmering taper's light,
> Adorns and cheers the way."

Our meals were brought us from a restaurant in the town, and we ate, like our soldiers, picnic style, and drank our coffee from the humble tin cup. After breakfast a cry was heard, "A boat, a boat!" And very soon, to our great delight, the beautiful steamboat, "Mattie Wayne," came into view. On it we took passage at once for St. Louis. The boat was splendid in every way and the fare was sumptuous. There was only one thing to make me uncomfortable during my stay on this beautiful steamer, and that was seeing the chambermaid, a neat looking white woman, sit down to the table to take her meals in company with the black men who were waiters on the boat. I had never seen anything like it before. We loved our black servants, but they always had their dining table separate. The idea of seeing a white woman sit down to the table to eat with these black men was shocking to me.

On arriving at St. Louis we changed boats and were soon ascending the muddy waters of the Missouri River. At last Kansas City was reached, but before we landed on the shore, the news of war reached our ears. The greatest excitement prevailed. Men, coming from every quarter, formed themselves into an army to expel a band, whose leaders were Brown, of Harper's Ferry renown, and a man by the name of Lane. This band was marching from home to home destroying property, and even burning down houses and turning women and children out homeless on the prairies, because of difference in politics. They too were interested as to how the Territory should come into the

Union, hence were using these means for the accomplishment of their purpose.

We went to a hotel in a small place called Westport, now swallowed up in the great city called Kansas City. Mr. Clayton and his men at once offered their services to these Missourians who were determined to put a stop to the outrages being committed by these disturbers of the peace. They immediately went into camp equipped as rough soldiers with red flannel shirts, corduroy pants, canteens, cartridge boxes, and so forth.

Refugees from homes on the prairies filled almost every house, and I heard grey-headed women tell sad tales of the annoyances they had received at the hands of this lawless band. The women and children of our party were all provided for at the hotel. The first night, my husband said to me:

"Victoria, I dislike to leave you, very much, but should I stay with my wife the men would think that they should be allowed the same privilege."

Being their captain made it more imperative that he do his whole duty, consequently he shared the camp with them.

Before leaving me, however, he taught me how to use a pistol should it become necessary. The pistol he gave me was loaded and ready for use. I slept with this instrument of death under my pillow for weeks. My room at the hotel opened on a veranda, and on that veranda numbers of these rough soldiers were sleeping. All the surroundings were appalling to any one, particularly to a gently nurtured woman.

My door had no fastening, so I drew my trunk up against it to keep it closed, placed my trust in an Almighty Father, and prayed as the sweet Psalmist of Israel once did: "Be merciful unto me, O God, be merciful unto me: for my soul trusteth in Thee: yea, in the shadow of Thy wing will I make my refuge, until these calamities be overpast." I laid me down to sleep and awoke next morning refreshed from the unmolested slumbers of the night.

It was so unpleasant, however, at this public place that I said to Mr. Clayton after we had breakfasted:

"Do get me board in a quiet family in which I may remain while you are away in camp, or perhaps battle."

He sent out one of his men to canvass the surrounding country to procure a temporary home for two ladies and myself. He was gone many hours and returned, saying every house was already filled.

I then asked permission to go in search of a place myself, as I thought I could plead our cause successfully. His reply was:

"Get your hat, we will go."

In the distance we saw a large brick house situated between Kansas City and the little village of Westport. A walk of about a mile through the sweet morning air brought us to the stone steps of this building. On them Mr. Clayton sat down, and motioned me to enter. I was met at the door by a middle aged woman, who invited me in very kindly. I at once told her my business. Whereupon she said:

"I regret that my rooms are all occupied, therefore will be obliged to turn you away."

I laid before her the whole situation and said:

"It looks hard that we ladies, so many hundred miles from our homes and friends, while our husbands are going out to defend your homes and property, cannot procure a safe and comfortable place to remain in during their stay in the army."

Her woman's heart was touched by this appeal, so she said:

"My dining room is quite large. Come and see if you ladies can accommodate yourselves there. If so, I will move my dining table into my own bed room and thus spare the dining room to you."

I found it large and airy, detached somewhat from the main building. I thanked her and accepted the kind offer. We were very soon domiciled in our new apartments. One of the ladies, Mrs. Reynolds, was a Massachusetts woman, who had came South as a teacher and married a printer in Georgia. She had no children. The other lady was a Southern woman, Mrs. Snow, from Alabama, and she had five little children. This made a large number to occupy one apartment. However, "Necessity is the mother of invention," so we very soon, with the use of curtains, had two apartments instead of one. Mrs. Snow, with her little children occupied one, and Mrs. Reynolds and myself the other.

Before the last farewells were said preparatory to going in quest of the enemy, the men entrusted their treasures to my keeping; the largest and most valuable being the thousands of dollars designed for the purpose of buying lands and settling the families which had come from the far South to make their homes in Kansas. This money I wore around my waist, but I was so careful to conceal this valuable girdle that my room-mate knew not of its presence until the return of the men and the delivery of it to them. Many little keepsakes were also in my keeping. Among the various articles was a

Masonic badge given me by a Mason. On entrusting it to me he said:

"Mrs. Clayton, in the event we are killed and you left in sorrow, find a Mason, show him this, tell him of your trouble, and you will surely find a friend."

I guarded these precious things each night with a loaded pistol under my pillow.

This was my first experience with the terrible thing called war, but, oh, not my last. The men were for some days quartered miles out on the prairie preparing for the conflict. Here I made my first visit to a military camp. As this army advanced, the enemy fell back, and there were only a few skirmishes with the loss of a few men, when several thousand United States troops, under command of Gen. Gary, arrived. Some of the Missourians joined this command, and very soon comparative peace was restored.

We found our land-lady exceedingly courteous and kind to us. She had vast apple orchards laden with fruit to which we had unlimited access, and we always had some of the choicest fruit, gathered with loving hands, ready for the enjoyment of our good men when they could get off from camp to make us a visit.

After peace was restored sufficiently, Mr. Clayton selected and purchased lands, wagons, horses, oxen, etc., and saw each family provided with the necessaries for the making of a comfortable home. In return for this they were to cast their votes for the interest, as we then thought, of our beloved South. The object of our journey being accomplished, we wished to see the country. So Mr. Clayton procured a small wagon and a pair of mules. Luckily, the wagon was provided with springs, otherwise our riding would have been very fatiguing.

In company with Mr. Clayton's assistant, Mr. Danforth, and a young man from Montgomery, Mr. Reed, we started out to see this great country, going to Lecompton first. The hotel there was being built, the outer walls up, and the roof covered, but no partitions dividing the rooms were finished. The room assigned Mr. Clayton and myself was divided off by means of pieces of carpet and matting hung around. The windows had sashes, but no glass. We remained here several days, and were awakened one night by what the natives called a Norther, the wind blowing and howling and the building shaking. Just think of it, not a pane of glass in either window! We managed to get through the dark hours by pulling the bed clothes over our heads. Next morning it would have been laughable to one to have seen us looking for the clothes we had deposited on the chairs the previous night. We finally gathered our garments together, and made our toilet as well as circumstances would allow. It was so cold that I repaired to the kitchen after breakfast to get warm. Fortunately this cold spell was of short duration. The vegetables here were abundant and delicious.

While in Lecompton, an old citizen of Alabama, a rough countryman, Mr. Blake Justus, who had moved here some two years previous, hearing that we were in town, came to see us. I had never met the old man before. I was introduced to him and he thus addressed me:

"Well, Madam, this is a fine country on men and horses, but h—ll on women and oxen."

I thought from observation that he was very near right.

We visited a number of towns and saw fine crops growing all along the road. The corn was so thick in the rows that it appeared to have been sown instead of dropped, as we were accustomed to see.

In Tecumseh the inhabitants seemed to be afflicted with chills. I saw several children in the same bed shaking at the same time, and in a few hours they were up eating water-melons.

The lands appeared to be exceedingly productive, but, oh, the powerful winds that swept over these vast prairies! I heard a man say that he could put his hand behind him and feel the wind blowing entirely through him. The people who lived there said it was with difficulty they kept locks on their doors on account of the winds.

On our return to the borders of

Missouri, we stopped some little time in the town of Lawrence, and we judged the time of our arrival must have been the weekly baking day from the display of pies, bread, and other good things taken from the oven.

In passing through the Territory we observed quite a number of white men with Indian squaws for wives. I presumed that they had gone out to the reservation and married these women for their lands.

I recall one peculiar incident in our experience with the Indians. We had occasion to go into the house of one of these people on the roadside to rest while the mules were being fed. It was a kind of public house, I suppose. In the apartment we entered there were about a dozen men and women sitting around. They said not a word, but bowed their heads and went out, one by one, until we were quite alone.

When we reached Kansas City on our return, we called at our former boarding house to bid our kind friends adieu.

The month of October had come, and we saw the fruits of this country in the bountiful gathering harvest. Mrs. Evans, our land-lady, sent her apples to distant markets for sale, but not until they were dried. The negroes brought them in from the orchards by wagon loads and stored them in cellars. After supper a basket-full would be brought into the sitting-room, and the children would peal, core and slice them ready for drying. And in this way they were prepared for market.

The soil around Kansas City was fine and quite black. After a rain it was very slippery. Mrs. Reynolds and I went out to walk after a shower one day, and thought we would descend a hill hunting a spring, as we had just seen a boy coming from that direction with a pail of water on his head. A peculiarity of our negroes was to carry all burdens on their heads — something a white person is unable to do. When we reached the brow of the hill and started to go down, we traveled with more velocity than we had ever done before, and in a few minutes reached the bottom, not, however, without leaving the marks of our feet and hands all the way. You may be sure, we were two astonished women. On our return we had to put our ingenuity to work to get up to the point we had started from. The ladies laughed heartily at us and insisted that I should become a border ruffian, as also Mrs. Reynolds; for they thought we could so well adapt ourselves to circumstances.

Here the fires were made of walnut wood. I went into the kitchen and saw the old colored aunty trying to kindle her fire by whittling up this wood into splinters, and I said to her, "Aunty, if you were in Alabama you could get what we call fat splinters, and soon have a great blaze crackling in your stove." She had never heard of lightwood or fat splinters before. I explained that it was pine wood full of turpentine and that was why it burned so readily. All their fires were of wood, as they had not commenced the use of coal.

V.

RETURN TO ALABAMA—HOME INCIDENTS—MUTTERINGS OF WAR—INCIDENTS AT PENSACOLA—EXTEMPORE MANUFACTURING.

MR. CLAYTON, Mr. Danforth, and I, finally said good-bye to our friends, and took passage in a boat for St. Louis. We were in St. Louis several hours and spent the time sightseeing. As it was Saturday afternoon, one of the most interesting experiences we had was going through the market beholding the great variety and quantity of food designed for consumption on the ensuing Sunday.

We left St. Louis with pleasant impressions, and resumed our journey towards home. When we landed at Memphis, Tenn., it seemed almost like home to us. The manners, customs, and even the pronunciation of words were unlike those of the Western friends we had recently left. At Memphis we took the stage to Huntsville, Ala. We reached Huntsville just at the break of day. After the slow, tedious ride of the past night we indeed felt glad at the sight of the "iron horse" once more. Our fast travel by the railroad soon brought us home.

When we finally caught the familiar view of our dear home we were constrained to exclaim with one of our Southern poets:

"Land of the South—imperial land—
How proud thy mountains rise!
How sweet thy scenes on every hand—
How fair thy evening skies!
But not for this—oh! not for these—
I love thy fields to roam:
Thou hast a dearer spell for me,
Thou art my native home!"
—*Judge Meek.*

We found things getting along as well as we anticipated. The negroes were overjoyed at our return. Faithful old Joe had been true to his duty, and his wife, Nancy, had taken care that "Mistus" should find everything about the house and yard neat, clean, and in order on her return after the long, long absence.

We at once resumed the old routine of daily duties, but my husband soon made manifest the malaria absorbed in his system during our sojourn in the West, by having chills; and before he was cured I was taken ill with continued fever, and for many weeks was a sufferer. Nancy nursed me tenderly through all the long tiresome nights.

Next spring a son was born to us, this making us three living children.

Mr. Clayton was noted for his hospitality and would often bring gentlemen home without giving me notice, knowing that I had plenty in the larder and a willing heart to provide for all who came. On one occasion I remember he went into Eufaula, met some gentlemen, about a half dozen in number, going out to look at the country with a view to extending the railroad from Eufaula to Clayton, and invited them to our home. He returned with them all, leaving Eufaula early in the morning with no breakfast but a cup of coffee, and then making an excursion of twenty-one miles. They reached our home about ten o'clock, tired and hungry. Mr. Clayton came to me and said:

"Victoria, make ready for the comfort of these gentlemen. They have had no breakfast."

My cook needed only to be told that Master had brought friends and wished a good breakfast prepared as quickly as possible; nothing afforded her more pleasure. In a short time the table was spread with many dishes to tempt the hungry gentlemen. It was the time of summer fruits, and nothing could be more appetizing in the morning than such freshly gathered, and nothing more refreshing than fragrant flowers covered with dew, filling the dining-room with beauty and grateful perfume. The gentlemen expressed themselves very much delighted with the cordial welcome extended them.

In entering upon our married life and coming to our little cottage home, we were invited the first night to take tea with our nearest neighbor. The lady of the house was not expecting strangers to come to share family tea, and she made many apologies, which embarrassed us, as they showed us that she was uncomfortable. This was a good object-lesson to a newly married wife. Since that night I have always endeavored to make our guests feel easy by offering no apology, but doing the best I could. Persons ordinarily do not come to see one so much for the food they find as for social enjoyment, and they always appreciate a heartfelt welcome.

The young men of our town would often send out to say:

"Mrs. Clayton, we wish to have a social gathering of the young people to-night. May we come to your house?"

The reply was always:

"Come, but come early that you may retire early."

I always gave them refreshments. If too late to bake cake, I would give them cold ham, light bread, pickles, hot coffee, etc. When the guests came they were told that whenever they wished refreshments they could find them in the dining-room, and there was a ser-vant to wait on them. I believe the servants enjoyed these informal gatherings as much as I did.

Assiduous attention to business, and the desire to lay up something for the education of our children and the winter of old age, kept my husband out of public affairs until induced by his friends to represent the County of Barbour in the Legislature. In 1857 he was elected to the Legislature without opposition, and was re-elected in 1859. Whenever he was absent from home I remained to manage our children and the slaves. It was while he was serving his country as a Legislator that the mutterings of the terrible war storm came to us.

We of the South felt that we had become slave-holders under our common government with its most sacred sanction, and, being an agricultural people, our property consisted mostly of slaves. Our Northern brethren were a manufacturing people, their property consisting of factories of various kinds, likewise with the most sacred sanction of our common government. We of the South looked to this, our common government for the protection of our property, and felt that we did not receive this protection. Things had come to such a pass that when a delicate woman of the South wished to travel through the Northern States to recuperate her health, she dared not take her servant nurse to attend her for the fear of having her taken away because she was a slave. Yet the government permitted her to own that slave as property. Thus we were made to feel as felt and said Patrick Henry in reply to exactions of the British upon the colonies:

"There no longer is any room for hope. We must fight. I repeat it, sir, we must fight. An appeal to arms and the God of battle is all that is left us."

"Had the South permitted her property, her constitutional rights, and her liberties to be surreptitiously taken from her without resistance and made no moan, would she not have lost her honor with them? If the alternative were between such a loss and armed resistance, is it surprising that she preferred the latter?"*

These feelings and principles had descended to us from Jefferson and Madison, and had come down baptized in the blood of heroes of 1776.

At this juncture, January, 1861, while Mr. Clayton was in the Legislature and on the Committee of the Military, Gov. Moore issued a call for twelve months' volunteers to go to Pensacola to relieve those who had been sent there to capture the Navy Yard and Forts Barancas and McRee. At the instance of the Clayton Guards and

---
*R. M. T. Hunter.

the Eufaula Rifles, he obtained their acceptance by Gov. Moore as a part of the force then called for. He had been Captain of the former, and both of these companies composed a part of the then Third Regiment of Alabama Volunteer Corps, of which he was at that time the Colonel. Gov. Moore declined to accept the entire Regiment, although every company tendered its services, for the reason that two regiments only being called for, he wished to receive companies from all parts of the State. The two companies went into camp at Eufaula on the 17th day of January, 1861. Col. Clayton obtained leave of absence from the Legislature, and received instructions from the Governor to bring them together at Montgomery.

He came home to say good-bye to loved ones, and to tell the negroes to take care of his family and to be faithful while he should be gone. The next day he returned to the command at Eufaula, going from thence to Montgomery, where, on the 12th day of February, the companies were formally mustered into the military service of the State of Alabama for twelve months. Seeing that he could not prevail on the Governor to accept the regiment, he was himself mustered in as a private in the Clayton Guards, believing this to be his duty.

The Governor, seeing that he was determined to go, regardless of the appeals that he could not be spared from the Legislature, on the following day sent him a commission as Aide-de-Camp with instructions to take command of the Alabama volunteers near Pensacola, and organize them into a regiment as fast as the required number of companies should arrive. Upon the organization of the First Alabama Regiment, on the 28th of March, he was elected Colonel.

"These soldiers, many of them, were our distinguished citizens, such as Hons. James L. Pugh, John Cochran, E. C. Bullock, and others. The prompt and faithful discharge of all the duties of private soldiers by these gentlemen, and their earnest support of the Colonel in his trying ordeal of enforcing discipline among those with whom he had been accustomed to associate upon terms of equality and familiarity, were in the highest degree complimentary to themselves and to him. They would never allow themselves to be relieved of any duty which fell to their lot, whether on guard, throwing up works, or mounting cannon. Their cheerful compliance with all orders, and the influence which their examples exerted in stilling the complaints of others, can only be properly appreciated when we remembered that the regiment was composed largely of the very first gentlemen of the country, who had been suddenly called together in a military camp, in the expectation of a battle; and instead of fighting, except the battle of Santa Rosa, and two bombardments, they were kept almost a year in digging in the sand among the fleas and mosquitoes on the Gulf coast."*

The Colonel, Mr. Clayton, was quartered in the house formerly occupied by the Federal officer, Col. Slemmer, who was then in command over at Fort Pickens.

In March I went down to visit the soldiers, and found that several of our ladies had preceded me and were already occupying houses in the Navy Yard. Here we had the pleasure of seeing our husbands quite frequently, and spent several months pleasantly in

---
Public Men of Alabama.—Garrett.

this beautiful place. To every house belonged a garden, and every garden was filled with lovely flowers, roses, geraniums, and many bright little annuals. Those sweet balmy spring days! How little did we realize the sorrow in store for us and for our whole country!

One day an old Irish woman came to bring the Colonel a pair of gloves she had made for him, and she said to me:

"This will be settled without any more bloodshed. I had my clothes out on the line yesterday, and drops of blood fell from the heavens on them, and I know this will be all the blood poured out in this war."

Poor, simple creature, how badly mistaken she was!

I remained at the Navy Yard until June. All of our ladies made frequent visits to the army so near by, oftentimes taking dinner with the soldiers, who would always have something nice served according to camp custom. They procured almost everything they wanted in the way of eatables from Pensacola. Our supply of luxuries had not been exhausted so early in the war. Soldiers were not provided, however, with many things deemed indispensable to us at home, such as white table cloths.

One day Gov. Moore was expected to arrive for a review of the troops, and all the ladies were invited to dine with him at the Colonel's quarters. This being an extra occasion, the table was graced with a white cloth and loaded with a splendid dinner, comprising almost every variety of good things that the Pensacola market afforded, well prepared and nicely served. We had not noticed the material of the cloth, but after dinner was over, Mr. Johnston, the Quartermaster, said to the boy who waited on us:

"Bob, where did you get your table

cloth to-day? I did not know that we were supplied with such a luxury."

He whispered:

"Mars' Lee, them is the Colonel's sheets."

These pleasant days, like all earthly things, were soon to come to an end.

From appearances over at Fort Pickens one night, a bombardment was anticipated, and all the camp was in the greatest excitement. Every woman was up and dressed and ready to take her departure towards Pensacola. During this excitement Mr. Johnston, who was Quartermaster, came to me with a quantity of gold money (having received it to pay the soldiers) to be entrusted to me for safe keeping. It was enclosed in a buckskin case and I fastened it around my waist. This was the second time in my life that I had the responsibility of wearing so valuable a girdle.

This time, as before, no one shared the knowledge of its presence with me.

Next day we went over to Pensacola, and rooms were procured for us at the hotel. There we remained but a short time, occasionally enjoying the privilege of seeing the gentlemen from across the bay. During our stay some ladies came down for the purpose of visiting the army. They went around through the country in a carriage to the camp, where they found so much to see and to interest them that they were unconscious of the flight of time; and, ere they knew it, night was near at hand, making it impossible for them to return that night to Pensacola. Consequently they were compelled to remain in camp until morning. The dear, unselfish, thoughtful soldiers soon had beds furnished them. They even remembered that the ladies were unprovided with night robes, and furnished them with some of their freshly-laundered night apparel as substitutes. Who would have expected men to think of so small a comfort, and so readily to improvise the means of supplying the want?

I returned in June to our home which I had left entirely in the care of negroes. My husband's brother, whom we had left there on going to Kansas, was now in the army at Pensacola. Not a white face was on the plantation. Everything had been entrusted to old Joe, the foreman, and Nancy, his wife. Joe looked after the work, stock, etc., and Nancy had my keys, attending to giving rations out, feeding all, and particularly to nursing the sick. She had no education except the knowledge of figures, and she could discern the time by clock or watch. She was particularly gifted with good, common sense, and was a most valuable help to me in the family, being at the same time a trusty servant and a friend. Everything was moving on satisfactorily as I anticipated. All the negroes came to greet me with many exclamations of joy at my return.

I then had to begin a new occupation—cloth-making. Our ports were all closed and we could have no intercourse with the outside world, consequently everything we needed to eat or to wear had to be made at home. No time was spent in idle speculation, but I went to work in good earnest trying to do as the wise man said: "She looketh well to the ways of her household, and eateth not the bread of idleness."

Just as I had become deeply immersed in my new occupation I received a telegram:

"The Colonel is sick. Come nurse him."

This was in August. My babe, a little girl of twelve months, I left with my friends and started off with an anxious heart. On reaching the army, I found Mr. Clayton very sick with typhoid fever. He was not in the Marine Hospital with the other sick soldiers, but in the Surgeon's apartments near by. Dr. Johnston, one of the Medical Corps, had him moved into his private room, where I found him tenderly cared for by the doctors. I took my place as nurse by his bedside and kept it for many weeks. I was not so engrossed, however, with my patient but that I could occasionally visit some poor boy in the hospital, taking a nice delicacy to remind him of his distant home and dear mother. I was and always will be under lasting obligations to these gentle doctors for their kindness to us.

As soon as my patient was sufficiently convalescent I carried him home, and we were very much delighted to see all the slaves so rejoiced that God had spared him. As soon as he recovered his strength he returned to his post of duty, and I saw him no more until November, when I received a notice that he had been sent to Mobile to hold a Court Martial, and would probably remain there some days, and wished to have me meet him there.

It was an exceedingly busy time with us when the news came. We were hauling the sugar-cane in from the fields and having it made into syrup and sugar; so we sat up all night to finish this work. I then made preparations and left for Mobile.

At Montgomery I met a friend, who kindly assisted me by sending a telegram to Col. Clayton, telling him that I was on my way, so that he could meet me on my arrival at Mobile. I traveled by rail until about midnight, when we reached the State line; and I was then obliged to take a coach for Blakely on the Mobile Bay. It was exceedingly dark, but, with the kind help of a gentleman, I succeeded in getting a seat in the coach. There were many other passengers, all gentlemen. During the night the voices of some of these gentlemen seemed very familiar to me, but I said nothing. When morning came they proved to be friends I had met on my mission of mercy to the army in August. When we reached Blakely we got breakfast, and took steamer across the Bay for Mobile.

On arriving, I saw Mr. Clayton on the wharf waiting to receive me. His business in Mobile consumed a week or more. He then returned to his post of duty and I to mine.

Never for one moment did we entertain the idea of the possibility of losing our cause. We were full of patriotism, and willing to make any sacrifices for our country. Alas! How little did we think we would eventually be called on to submit, and to give up the results of our labor for all these years of our young lives, and in old age to feel privation!

Upon the expiration of the term of service of this regiment, Col. Clayton was requested by nearly all of the officers in it to re-organize it and retain the command. Fearing that, as it had become so well drilled in heavy artillery, it would be kept upon post duty, and himself desiring a more active field, he yielded the re-organization of the regiment to Lieutenant Colonel Stedman. He returned home and went up to his old native county of Chambers, now Lee, where his boyhood days had been spent, and where he had worked side by side with his father's negroes, he taking charge of the plow hands and his brother Joe the hoe hands; not in the capacity of overseers only, but working as well. There, too, he had gone hunting with these same negro boys, and many a fat opossum had they treed and brought home together. Here, where every scene brought to remembrance some pleasant bygone, he called for men to organize a regiment for the service of the State. Men came in from all the surrounding counties, and ere many weeks had elapsed, his regiment was ready for service, and was accepted as the Thirty-ninth Alabama.

While the men were preparing for the army, my mother-in-law came in every morning from her home, to Opelika, where they were stationed; and she, with the help of the ladies of the town, worked on the uniforms for our soldiers. The clothes had been made by the tailors, but the ladies put on all the insignia, stripes, etc. Every lady in the land was enthusiastic to do all in her power to help. All were full of patriotism. We do not regret this now, and it will be a source of gratification to our Southern women as long as they live, and an inheritance to their children.

> "Breathes there a man with soul so dead,
> Who never to himself hath said
> This is my own, my native land?"

Mr. Clayton's regiment was now ready for service. He came to say the final good-bye before entering into the bloody contest. Our children then numbered five, and all gathering round him and kneeling down, he committed us to the care of an almighty and loving Father. This sad good-bye! No one could conceive of its depths of sadness, except those who have experienced the like.

This same regiment Col. Clayton commanded in Bragg's Kentucky campaign until after the battle of Murfreesboro, in which he was seriously wounded in the right shoulder. Here his brother, Joseph Clayton, who commanded a company in the same regiment, was mortally wounded. After the battle our army fell back, and Capt. Joseph Clayton was necessarily left in the hands of the enemy. Every provision possible was made for his comfort. He was placed in a small house in a lady's yard, and this lady promised to do all she could for him.

Col. Clayton came home on furlough, suffering much from his wound. He did not linger in the happiness of home and loved ones long, but hastened back to his command, still suffering from his wound, and on arriving was surprised by the delivery to him of a commission as Brigadier-General. He at once took charge of a brigade composed of the Eighteenth, Thirty-sixth, Thirty-eighth, Thirty-second, and Fifty-eighth Alabama regiments all combined, and assigned to the division of Major-General A. P. Stewart.

It is unnecessary to speak of the part taken by Clayton's brigade in the campaign and battles that followed. Suffice it to say, that the conduct of the brigade and its commanding officer in the battles of Chickamauga, Rocky Face Mountain, and New Hope Church, brought to the latter a higher commission—that of Major-General.

The sad news of Capt. Clayton's condition reached his mother, and she, her strong mother's love bearing her up, started in company with her daughter to seek him. After several days' travel, they reached the Confederate forces under Gen. Bragg, who sent them on as far as his picket line in an ambulance. They then walked until they got into the line of the Federal forces in command of Gen. Rosecrans. The earth was enveloped in the darkness of night, which, if possible, made it more trying to these ladies. The officer they met treated them kindly, giving them seats by the camp fire. They related the mission which had brought them, unprotected as they were, so far from home and friends and into the lines of the enemy. The officer immediately sent a courier to the General to know if the ladies should be permitted to seek the wounded man. This answer came quickly: "Put the ladies out immediately."

The kind officer who had received them, I know had a mother, a sister, or, perhaps, a wife, whom he loved, and his memory of them made him extend the hospitality of the camp fire to these poor "Pilgrims of the Night." He said:

"Ladies, I cannot turn you out into the darkness, but will permit you to remain by the camp fire till morning."

They were very grateful in accepting his kindness. When the light of day greeted them they began their sorrowful retreat. After walking some distance, they came to a country home, which they entered, and, as soon as the inmates of the house knew who they were, they were invited in to share the family meal.

After the meal was ended and the ladies were taking a much needed rest, they were aroused by a great noise and commotion around the premises. On going out on the veranda they soon discovered the cause of all this excitement. A foraging party from the Federal army was filling their wagons with every kind of country produce they could find, some men in the smoke-house throwing out the meat, some running down and catching pigs, turkeys, chickens, etc., some in the dairy trying to consume all of its contents, several trying to drink out of one milk vessel at the same time. After searching and procuring all they wanted, the wagons were sent on, and the officers in command came into the house where the ladies were, and asked the young ladies for some music on the piano, and a song. This reminds me of what David said of the Israelites when they had been taken captive: "By the rivers of Babylon, there we sat down, yea, we wept, when we remembered Zion. We hanged our harps upon the willows in the midst thereof. For there they that carried us away captive required of us a song; and they that wasted us required of us mirth, saying, Sing us one of the songs of Zion."

While there, the officer saw this old mother and asked of her the cause of her distress. She told him of her sorrow. He manifested considerable interest in her, saying, "Madam, be comforted; I will seek your son and write you of him, and bring the letter here to this lady, who will get the letter through to you." She then gave him full particulars where to find her son in Murfreesboro.

The old woman was exceedingly touched with his kind sympathy, and after her return home watched anxiously for the expected news from her son, lying in pain and suffering among strangers. The promised letter at last came, and made the hearts of the whole family rejoice, because it said that the Captain was getting well. This joy did not last long, for very soon the surgeon in charge of him came to tell the family that he had died ten days after being left by our army. I hope this officer did not intentionally wound these people by his erroneously favorable report, but was mistaken as to the man.

VI.

HOME TRIALS AND LABORS—CLOTH-MAKING — VARIOUS ILLUSTRATIVE INCIDENTS.

WHILE my husband was at the front doing active service, suffering fatigue, privations, and the many ills attendant on a soldier's life, I was at home struggling to keep the family comfortable.

We were blockaded on every side, could get nothing from without, so had to make everything at home; and having been heretofore only an agricultural people, it became necessary for every home to be supplied with spinning wheels and the old-fashioned loom, in order to manufacture clothing for the members of the family. This was no small undertaking. I knew nothing about spinning and weaving cloth. I had to learn myself, and then to teach the negroes. Fortunately for me, most of the negroes knew how to spin thread, the first step towards cloth-making. Our work was hard and continuous. To this we did not object, but our hearts sorrowed for our loved ones in the field.

CARDING AND WEAVING.

Our home was situated a mile from the town of Clayton. On going to town one day I discovered a small bridge over which we had to pass that needed repairing. It was almost impassable. I went home, called some of our men, and gave them instructions to get up the necessary articles and put the bridge in condition to be passed over safely. I was there giving instructions about the work, when an old gentleman, our Probate Judge, came along. He stopped to see what we were doing. When satisfied, he said to me:

"Madam, I think we will never be conquered, possessing such noble women as we do."

We believed our cause a righteous one, and that of course it would be crowned with success, but "Our Heavenly Father" was wiser than we.

There was no white person on the plantation beside myself and children, the oldest of whom was attending school in Eufaula, as our Clayton schools were closed, and my time was so occupied that it was impossible for me to teach my children. Four small children and myself constituted the white family at home.

I entrusted the planting and cultivation of the various crops to old Joe. He had been my husband's nurse in infancy, and we always loved and trusted him. I kept a gentle saddle horse, and occasionally, accompanied by Joe, would ride over the entire plantation on a tour of inspection. Each night, when the day's work was done, Joe came in to make a report of everything that had been done on the plantation that day. When Mr. Clayton was where he could receive my letters, I wrote him a letter every night before retiring, and in this way he, being kept informed about the work at home, could write and make suggestions about various things to help me manage successfully.

We made good crops every year, but after the second year we planted provision crops entirely, except enough cotton for home use.

All the coloring matter for cloth had to be gathered from the forest. We would get roots and herbs and experiment with them until we found the color desired, or a near approach to it. We also found out what would dye cotton and what woolen fabrics. We had about one hundred head of sheep; and the wool yielded by these sheep and the cotton grown in the fields furnished us the material for our looms. After much hard work and experience we learned to of our cloth being really pretty.

Our ladies would attend services in the church of God, dressed in their home-spun goods, and felt well pleased with their appearances; indeed, better pleased than if they had been dressed in silk of the finest fabric.

We made good warm flannels and other articles of apparel for our soldiers, and every woman learned to knit socks and stockings for her household, and many of the former were sent to the army.

In these dark days the Southern matron, when she sat down at night feeling that the day's work was over, took her knitting in her hands as a pastime, instead of the fancy work which ladies so frequently indulge in now.

I kept one woman at the loom weaving, and several spinning all the time, but found that I could not get sufficient cloth made at home; consequently I gave employment to many a poor woman whose husband was far away. Many a time have I gone ten miles in the country with my buggy filled with thread, to get one of these ladies to weave a piece of cloth for me, and then in return for her labor sent her syrup, sugar, or any of our home produce she wished.

We always planted and raised large crops of wheat, rice, sugar cane, and potatoes. In fact, we grew almost everything that would make food for man or beast. Our land is particularly blessed in this respect. I venture to say there is no land under the sun that will grow a greater variety of products than the land in these Southern states.

Being blockaded, we were obliged to put our ingenuity to work to meet the demands on us as heads of families. Some things we could not raise; for instance, the accustomed necessary luxury of every home—coffee. So we went to work to hunt up a substitute. Various articles were tried, but the best of all was the sweet potato. The potatoes were peeled, sliced, and cut into pieces as large as a coffee bean, dried, and then roasted just as we prepared coffee. This substitute, mixed with genuine coffee, makes a very palatable drink for breakfast. My supply of coffee was like the widow's barrel of meal we read of in the Bible, and it came to me in this way:

Just as the clouds of war became visible, Mr. Clayton laid in a large supply of coffee, and then, too, in the early days of the struggle, quite a number of ladies came to Clayton, refugees from New Orleans. The New Orleans people are noted for their fondness for good coffee, and these ladies were no exceptions to the rule. They brought a large quantity of it with them.

On our place we had the finest orchard in Southeast Alabama, and often generous baskets of luscious fruit were sent to these ladies, who were boarding in town at the hotel, and in return I would receive packages of coffee, and with frugality and economy in the using it lasted until the blockade became a thing of the past.

Another accustomed luxury of which we were deprived was white sugar. We had, however, a good substitute with which we soon became satisfied; our home-made brown sugar, from the sugar cane. It had the redeeming quality of being pure. One of my friends was going to be married, and wanted white sugar to frost the wedding cake. She came out to see if I had any on hand, as there was none to be bought. I told her that I regretted not having any, but could give her some of my brown sugar. I had frosted cakes with it many times. The frosting looked white and pretty at night, but slightly cream-colored in the day time. She accepted my offer, and I presume the guests never knew that the sugar used was not of the purest white.

We were very thankful to the beneficent Creator for all the blessings around us.

We made many gallons of wine from the scuppernong and other grapes every year. One year I remember particularly. Sheets were spread under the long scuppernong arbors, little negro boys put on top to throw the grapes down, and grown men underneath to gather them in baskets as they fell. When brought to the house they measured thirty-two bushels, and made one hundred and twenty gallons of wine. I did not make so large a quantity from the other varieties of grapes. This wine was kept in the cellar and used for the common benefit. When the negroes would get caught out in the rain, and come to the house wet, they did not hesitate to say, "Mistus, please give me a little wine to keep cold away;" and they always received it. There never was any ill result from the use of domestic wine. We were a temperate family and the use was invariably beneficial.

Closed in as we were on every side, with nearly every white man of proper age and health enlisted in the army, with the country filled with white women, children, and old, infirm men, make very comfortable clothing, some with thousands of slaves to be controlled, and caused through their systematic labor to feed and clothe the people at home, and to provide for our army, I often wonder, as I contemplate those by-gone days of labor and sorrow, and recall how peacefully we moved on and accomplished what we did.

We were required to give one-tenth of all that was raised, to the government. There being no educated white person on the plantation except myself, it was necessary that I should attend to the gathering and measuring of every crop and the delivery of the tenth to the government authorities. This one-tenth we gave cheerfully and often wished we had more to give.

My duties, as will be seen, were numerous and often laborious; the family on the increase continually, and every one added increased labor and responsibility. And this was the case with the typical Southern woman.

As I have before remarked, we never questioned that we were in the right, but thought that if we did our whole duty to God and our fellow man, whether our equal or a slave, a just God would reward us; and I believe that our reward is yet to come. We treated our slaves kindly, as fellow beings with like passions as ourselves, but as socially inferior to us, occupying the place of "hewers of wood and drawers of water." And during these four years of political darkness our slaves were faithful to us in all things of importance. Of course, in every family, however well

Various Incidents. 125

regulated, disturbances would sometimes occur. The negro women would occasionally get into dispute about their children, and even come to blows, and I would have to assert my authority to quell the outbreak and make peace; but I truly believe these negroes regarded their master and myself as their best friends, and really loved us.

They were not all good and honest like Joe and Nancy. Some were not to be trusted. Stealing was their great fault; usually something to eat. In my intercourse with them as mistress I tried to be mindful of their ignorance and weakness; and to realize how easily, like children, they would be tempted. Our Lord taught us to pray, "Lead us not into temptation," and I tried to shield them from it by sharing everything we had in the way of food with them, and providing them comfortable and neat clothing. In spite of all this care, however, they would sometimes break the eighth commandment.

One night during the war, or rather one morning just before the dawn of a Sunday, I heard a rap on the door, and a voice saying:

"Mistus, don't be frightened."

I arose and went to the door to know the cause of this unusual disturbance at this unearthly hour. There I found old Joe with one of the men. He said:

"Mistus, yer know somebody has been robbin' the apple orchard for several Sad'day nights. As I went down thar to see ef I could cetch the thief I hwerd a tappin at the beehive, and crept aroun' thar to see who it wuz and whut dey wuz up to; and when I grabbed der man, I found I hed Nat, one of our own folks, stealing honey."

I said:

"Why, Nat, when the honey was brought in last week, your wife came with the other women to receive a portion for your family, and now here you are, stealing more. You know you can get anything I have by asking for it. Why will you steal?"

He promised never to do so again, as he had promised many times before. However, Nat has made a tolerably good freeman, at least managing to keep out of the penitentiary.

I had also a negro woman who would steal, notwithstanding all my efforts to prevent it. She really loved me devotedly, and I was much attached to her. She would take every opportunity to pilfer, and many times carry off things she really had no use for. We had to make our medicine as well as other needful articles. Some one at Opelika, Alabama, had an establishment where castor oil was made. My father-in-law, coming to Clayton, brought me a bottle of the oil, which I was very glad to get for use in cases of sickness. I kept my medicines in a closet, and often in going in there to get medicine would leave the door unlocked, not supposing anyone would disturb medicine. This woman was one of my good spinners, consequently was in the house the greater portion of the day. She knew I had the bottle of oil. One day I had occasion to use it, and found, to my utter consternation, that some had been taken out of the bottle. I called up all the servants about the house to inquire if they knew anything about the missing oil. No one seemed to know anything about it. A few days after this, however, some thread was taken out of the spinning room, and, knowing her propensity, I told her that I believed she had taken it and it was my duty to look through her house for it. She went along with me, and very soon, in my search, I found a bottle concealed, and on examination it proved to be the lost castor oil. The thread I also found. I spoke kindly to her of her great sin in stealing, and she, as on numerous previous occasions, wept bitterly and promised never to do the like again.

Often similar unpleasant things would happen. Once a funny incident happened with my good woman, Nancy. We had a vast quantity of fine, very early peaches. She came to me to get permission to take a wagon load of them to sell. I consented, and furnished her with hands to help gather them. When she was ready to go, she washed and dressed up a little chap to go with her, to hold the horse whenever she went in to see if anybody wanted to buy peaches. Stopping in front of a lady's house, Dave was sent in to ask Mrs. Wise if she would take some fruit. The house was some little distance from the street.

He came back to the wagon, and as Nancy was driving off, Mrs. Wise called to her to stop; she said the boy had stolen some ornamental shells from around the door steps. Thereupon Nancy searched his pockets and questioned him as to whether he had taken them. He declared positively that he had not seen them. While driving down the next steet Nancy happened to look around at Dave. His hat was setting unusually high on his head. On removing it she found Mrs. Wise's shells deposited on his woolly locks; he was sitting there as complacently as though nothing had happened. This boy, since freedom, has spent a good portion of his time in the penitentiary for stealing.

Whenever one of our slaves was married, a sumptuous supper was always provided for the occasion, and when the weather was warm and suitable a table was spread out under the trees in the yard. Otherwise the supper was dispensed in the dining-room, and there they were allowed full liberty until supper was over. They enjoyed and always appreciated this attention very much.

These slaves were more like children than one would imagine. They were exempt from care more, I suppose, than any people on earth. Their owners providing for all their wants, they naturally took no thought for the morrow; and I believe as a whole they were the happiest class of laborers in the world.

Our Northern brethren heard only the bad side of slavery, and of course formed their ideas of the institution from these reports. I often felt that slavery was an evil, though I did not think it a sin. At any rate, it was established, and we were bound to do the best with it we could. I know the master was often too exacting with his slave, and in some instances unkindly so. His slave was his property, his money he had paid for him, and certainly he would do nothing to injure his value, any more than any man would injure his horse, cow, or any other piece of property. A healthy negro man was worth generally a thousand dollars, and his master would feel that it was to his interest to take care of that thousand dollars. To abuse it would be a loss to himself, even if he were not actuated by any more God-like motive. We sincerely wish our Northern brethren to give this matter some thoughtful consideration, and be disposed "Gently to hear and kindly to judge."

During the four years the war lasted, I made frequent visits to the army. I held myself in readiness to go at any time that a summons came from my good soldier husband. I kept my trunk packed with clothing bought in time of peace and reserved for extra occasions, and my little satchel hanging on the wall in my room, containing a bottle of brandy made from home fruits, medicine made from our Southern poppies, a paper of sugar, a candle, matches, etc. In my travels these articles were often brought into good service. Many a fellow traveler shared their comfort. If the summons came at midnight for me to go and see my absent one, I would leave in the early morning and travel twenty-one miles to catch the morning train at Eufaula. Before leaving, however, I would call in Joe and Nancy, and entrust the management of home to them. Nancy would take all my children over to one of my sisters who lived some two miles distant. The keys were left in Nancy's care to give out to Hannah the daily rations to cook for the negroes. If any were taken sick during my absence, the family physician, Dr. McNeil, was immediately called in, and they received every attention.

When the army was near Chattanooga, Tenn., I went in company with a gentleman, a citizen, who was going to make a visit to friends in the service. We reached the railroad station after nightfall when all was in darkness. Where to find accommodations for the remainder of the night we knew not. After climbing as well as we could into the depot we remained there until daylight. Notwithstanding the darkness the station was full of travelers. During our stay a woman said to me:

"Where are you going? To see your good man in the army?"

I replied, "Yes."

She then said:

"You leave your children at home?"

I told her, "Yes."

Then she asked, "Aren't you dhry? I have something and will give you a dhrink."

I thanked her, but declined her invitation. She was a good Irish woman, I suppose. It was so dark I could not see her.

Next morning we made our way to the army to see our friends. As the gentleman with me wore a long linen duster, having ceased to be fastidious about dress in those hard times, every side we turned we could hear the exclamation:

"Coat, where are you taking that man?"

These boys in grey had considerable fun at the expense of the man who wore the long-tail coat.

Another time I went up to spend some weeks in camp while the army was in winter quarters near Dalton, Georgia. Just after Christmas, Mr. Wood, who lived near us and was my husband's Quartermaster in the army, had come home on furlough. I returned to the army with him, taking Betsey, the wife of Ned, Mr. Clayton's cook. On reaching the army I found a cozy little log cabin ready to receive me. In it was a rudely constructed bedstead filled with hay, and covered over with bed clothes that had been carried from place to place in the marches, a table, a shelf, on which sat a bucket of water and a washpan, a few chairs and one of the largest fire-places I ever saw, filled with great logs of wood to warm up the entire house. Here in this rough little cabin I spent several weeks happily.

In coming I brought many comforts they were not provided with in camp—bed linen, table linen, etc.; and many luxuries in the way of food—sausages, coffee, all genuine, roasted and ground, sugar, cakes, etc. The officers' mess had been accustomed to only two meals a day—breakfast and dinner. Every evening I would have Betsey come into my cabin to make coffee and fix up such refreshments as we had, and invite the members of the mess to this humble abode to enjoy good cheer. Sometimes we would make a quantity of sugar candy and pull it white and nice to add to their pleasure. Thus passed many an evening with these soldier gentlemen during my stay.

One night we had a snow storm. We could feel the soft, white flakes gently falling on us during the night. Somehow they made their way through the roof, which was rain-proof. I had my ever-ready pastime along—my knitting —and employed my lonely moments, when the men were out on duty, knitting socks and reading *David Copperfield.*

While here, I attended religious worship in the open air, and, for the first time, saw one of our clergymen conduct the services with his spurs on and no robes. This clergyman was then Dr. Quintard, afterward Bishop of Tennessee. He was a very dear friend of Gen. Clayton. No man in the Confederate army did more good service than did Dr. Quintard. He, having been a practising physician, could go into the hospitals to minister to the unfortunates, physically as well as spiritually, and then preach to the more fortunate on Sunday.

BISHOP QUINTARD.

In February I returned home to find everything progressing as it should, except for one thing. Hannah, who was the cook for the field hands, concluded that she would make sassafras tea instead of the usual coffee. The hands had been clearing new ground, and brought a quantity of sassafras roots to the house, and she thought they would like a change. The use of this tea, I think, caused me to have several cases of pneumonia to nurse.

I was soon immersed in the old routine of duties, which were many. My children had to be looked after, and the welfare of our slaves, bodily and spiritually. We not only had the clothing to make from the wool and cotton we raised, but many other things had to be obtained, or substitutes found to take the place of them, as medicines, etc., etc.

These days of war and blockade tried our souls. Many a time when all the family were wrapped in slumber and all nature hushed in the silence of night, I have walked back and forth on the colonnade until the clock would toll out the midnight hour, thinking of dear absent ones. These were busy days and sad, sad nights to the Southern matron.

My last attempt to visit the army was attended with many difficulties and hardships. The long-continued, unequal struggle was telling on our people and country. When I reached Atlanta, orders had just been received from Gen. Bragg, saying, "Permit no citizens to pass, especially women." I was in trouble, not knowing what to do, or whither to go, when a kind gentleman said to me:

"Come, Mrs. Clayton, I think we can smuggle you into the car."

We started off, and on reaching the train found the entrance guarded by one of the soldiers. As soon as he found out I was Gen. Clayton's wife, and wished to go to the army, he permitted me to pass into the car without delay. I had a basket of good things along, and fed many a hungry soldier on the trip. That night I saw a nice-looking old gentleman, whom I recognized as dear old

Bishop Elliott, whose hands had been laid on my head in blessing many years before when I was a happy young girl. I told him that I was Victoria Hunter, when he at once remembered me as one of the girls educated under his superintendence at Montpelier. We enjoyed an hour in sweet conversation about the past. He was a holy servant of the Master, and one of the handsomest men I ever knew. When at college his fellow students called him Stephen the Magnificent, because of his handsome face and the benevolence beaming from his every feature.

When I arrived at Dalton the hotels were all closed, and it was almost night. Two other ladies besides myself were the only ladies that went from Atlanta in that long train of cars filled with soldiers. When we found no accommodations were to be had in Dalton we did not know what to do. Ned, my husband's cook, had been home on a furlough and I was taking him back; and, to add to my trouble, on arriving at Dalton Ned and my trunks were missing. I cannot say what we would have done had it not been for a minister who came up on the train with us and saw our situation. Mr. Ely, who proved to be a friend indeed, started off to find us a resting place, and soon returned to escort us to our respective places. I was fortunate in getting into the house of a Baptist preacher. He and his daughter, a sweet young lady, were very kind to me.

Next morning I went down to take the train for the army, and found, to my dismay, that it had been gone for some time, the schedule having been changed that very morning. Ned was there, however, with the luggage, all safe. A lady in Atlanta had lost her trunk and wanted mine to make up the

Various Incidents. 143

loss, and he being detained, was left until the next train. I was again at a loss whither to turn, but concluded best to go back to my new-found friends. Before many hours had passed, Mr. Ely, seeing a group of soldiers conversing, drew near them and discovered that Gen. Clayton was one of the number; he had left the army on a few days' furlough to recuperate his health, as he was quite unwell. Mr. Ely told him that I was in Dalton and brought him where I was. I proceeded no farther on my journey, but in company with my husband returned to Opelika, the home of his parents. I had taken one of my little boys along with me to show him the army. He was much disappointed that I went no further. Gen. Clayton remained with us about three days, then returned to his post of duty.

After this I never attempted another visit to the army. Times became too stormy for ladies to venture there. Rumors of Northern troops making raids and committing all kinds of depredations through the Southern states came to us frequently. Being so far south we were not disturbed by them until the war was almost ended. Our Postmaster, Mr. Petty, sent one morning in the ever-to-be-remembered spring, to let me know the startling news had been received that Gen. Grierson, with a detachment of Union soldiers, was passing through adjacent counties, and would probably reach Clayton very soon. I had old Joe called in and told him what had come. The old man seemed very much troubled. He said little, but that night, after all the family had retired and were wrapped in unconscious sleep, he came to consult me about secreting some provisions before the arrival of these hostile troops, fearing they might destroy these necessary articles and leave us in a state of want, as they had done in many instances. I said, "Well, Joe, you can do so if you wish."

He took his shovel and spade and went into the vegetable garden, which was quite large, as it furnished supplies for the entire family, white and colored. He began digging in good earnest and soon had a large opening made to receive the things, but could not finish it in one night. Fortunately, the garden was situated in an entirely different direction from the negro quarters, so that in going out to work next morning the hands did not discover the excavation that had been made in the night.

The next night he worked away until it was sufficiently large to hold what we thought necessary, then came to let me know that he was ready to make the transfer. With my basket of keys we went out to select the articles—bacon, sugar, syrup, wine, and many other things. After putting these things in the excavation, with hard work he covered them over, put earth on top until the great hole was entirely hid. Next morning after starting all to work he returned to the house, went into the garden, laid off the place where the things were hid in rows with a plow, and set out cabbage plants, so that in a few days they were growing as peacefully as though nothing but mother earth was resting beneath them. No one knew of this except Joe, his wife, Nancy, and myself, until peace was restored.

The scene was really amusing the day Joe called several of the men to assist him in restoring these numerous things to the places whence they had been taken so many weeks before. Removing the cabbage, opening the ground, and finding what was secreted there, was indeed a revelation to them, and their amazement was funny. They were curious to know when and how these things had gotten in there.

Annie, my house woman, said to me, when she knew the Yankees were coming:

"Mistus, give me your silver; I will take care of it until the Yankees are gone."

I told her to take it. One man took the gun, and so the valuables were divided out to these slaves for safe-keeping, and all proved faithful to the trust. The gold and silver money in the house I myself buried, in the dead of night, under a rose bush in my flower garden; and when our fears had been dissipated it was with some difficulty that I at last discovered its hiding place.

The day we knew the command would reach Clayton I instructed my cook, Nancy, to prepare the best and most abundant dinner possible, fearing that these Union soldiers would feel that they could with impunity treat me badly because my husband had taken so prominent a part in what they called the Rebellion. Knowing somewhat of human nature, I thought a good dinner would tend to conciliate them; but never did I mean to compromise my dignity as a lady of our fair Southland.

We were all excitement, expecting every moment to see the enemy come in sight. About noon the glittering bayonets were discerned in the distance. We watched with fear and trembling until the whole command had passed the road which turned towards our home, and not the face of one Yankee did we see. The reason they passed me by was explained to me afterwards. Col. Clark, one of our men who happened to be at home, with several others, went out some miles with a flag of truce

Brig. General Grierson, U. S. A.

to meet Gen. Grierson, and informed him of my unprotected situation, saying that he feared for me, as, being the wife of a Confederate General, some indignity on the part of the Union soldiers. Gen. Grierson, a true gentleman, as he was, immediately ordered a guard stationed at each road leading to our home, thereby leaving us unmolested. My husband always desired to thank this big-hearted General for the great kindness shown to his family in this trying hour, and at one time, on his way to California, he stopped over in the town where he understood Gen. Grierson lived to thank him in person, but was disappointed, as he learned that he was then absent from home. I shall always cherish the kindest feelings for Gen. Grierson, and pray that God will bless his family.

VII.

CLOSE OF THE WAR—INCIDENTS OF RECONSTRUCTION—EXTRACT FROM JUDGE CLAYTON'S CHARGE TO THE GRAND JURY—BEGINNING LIFE OVER.

VERY soon after this came news of the surrender, and that our beloved Confederacy was no more. This filled our land with sorrow. And I knew not where my General was. O, those terrible days of mourning and anxiety! I look back upon them as upon a dreadful nightmare. I was waiting, listening to every sound, fearing that something more terrible awaited us, when lo! once at the close of day I saw a man approaching on horseback. Wondering who this stranger was, and watching him closely until he reached the house, I found to my delight that he was our beloved lost one returned to us. My heart went out in thanksgiving and praise to an "Almighty and merciful Father" for the protection He had vouchsafed the loved one of our home through all the horrible vicissitudes of four years of bloodshed and war. His safe return was a miracle to me, for I knew that in every battle he entered he was always in the front ranks. He was as brave a soldier as the Confederate States had in their army. He was wounded twice, and in one battle came out on his fourth horse, two having been killed and one wounded under him. When he laid down the arms he had taken up for the Confederate States, the Union had no truer, more law-abiding citizen in all its area of country than was Henry DeLamar Clayton. Notwithstanding he had suffered much, he was willing to accept gracefully and patriotically the decisions of war, and devote himself earnestly and faithfully to the arts of peace, and thus add to the glory of his accepted country.

Ere long we received the anticipated intelligence that our slaves were all made free by the government of the United States. To this we bowed with submission. My husband said, "Victoria, I think it best for me to inform our negroes of their freedom." So he ordered all the grown slaves to come to him, and told them they no longer belonged to him as property, but were all free. He said to them, "You are not bound to remain with me any longer, and I have a proposition to make to you. If any of you desire to leave, in consideration of your faithfulness to my wife during the four years of my absence, I propose to furnish you with a conveyance to move you, and with provisions for the balance of the year."

The universal answer was, "Master, we want to stay right here with you."

The pleasure of knowing they were free seemed to be mingled with sadness. That very night, long after the usual hour for bedtime, the hum of the busy spinning wheel was heard. On inquiry in the morning I found that Nancy was the one spinning long into the night. Asking why she had been up so late at night at work, she replied:

"I have no master to feed and clothe Nancy now. She will have to look out for something for herself and look out for the rainy day."

In many instances slaves were so infatuated with the idea of being, as they said, "free as birds," that they left their homes and consequently suffered; but our slaves were not so foolish.

We had the cotton crop on hand

which was made the first year of the war. After that year we had planted only provisions, and no cotton except for the clothing of the family. This old cotton crop was sold, and the proceeds divided out among all; each family receiving according to its size. Just at this time a merchant received a lot of dry goods, the first store-bought goods we had seen in Clayton for four years. Everybody went to look at the goods. Our negroes soon parted with their money. Some bought judiciously, some gay finery. All were pleased.

My brother had a man named John, a brick mason by trade, to whom he was very much attached. He said to him:

"John, you are free."

He replied:

"Massa, I'd like to see them Yankees make me eny freer den I is."

John continued to take his earnings to his master as long as he could work, and when sickness and old age found him the family nursed him tenderly until death claimed him, and then they felt that a friend had gone.

Gen. Clayton devoted himself to his farm, the only difference in the order of things being that the former slaves were paid monthly wages, and provided their own clothes. I often said to my husband that the freedom of the negroes was a freedom to me, a freedom from responsibility and care.

We lived this way for a few years. Then Gen. Clayton was made Circuit Judge, and this necessitated his being absent from home the greater part of the year, and he could not give such attention to the farm as to make it profitable. Consequently he told the negroes he could hire them no longer, but permitted some of them to have farms on the plantation, they taking the responsibility and paying part of the crop to him. They began then to scatter, but some of the old slaves have been with us all the years until now.

Gen. Clayton was elected Judge of the Eighth Judicial District of Alabama in 1866, which position he held until July, 1868, when he was removed under the Reconstruction Acts of Congress. His charge to the Grand Jury, in Pike County, a portion of which related to the condition of our country, to the treatment of our former slaves, and to the spirit which ought to animate the people, was published by the unanimous request of the Bar, and it was republished North and South as a campaign document. I think it not out of place to insert a portion of it here, together with the following request on the part of the Bar for its publication:

"TROY, ALABAMA, Sept. 11, 1866.
"The undersigned members of the

Bar of Pike County, having heard with much satisfaction and approval your charge to the Grand Jury of Pike County, and being convinced that the publication of that part of your charge which concerns the relations between the white population and the negroes lately emancipated would have a good effect upon the Country, respectfully ask for a copy of the same for publication.

"A. N. Worthy,
"W. C. Wood,
"W. C. Oates,
"J. D. Gardner,
"W. H. Parks,
"W. B. Roberts,
"Benj. Gardner,
"G. T. Yelverton,
"E. L. McIntyer,
"H. C. Semple,
"J. C. Flournoy,
"J. N. Arrington,

"Ham McIntyer,
"John P. Hubbard,
"N. W. Griffin."

Extract from the charge of Judge Clayton to the Grand Jury of Pike County on the 9th day of September, 1866, and published by request of the Bar and the Grand Jury in their general Presentments.

"There is a class of our population clothed with certain civil rights and privileges which they did not possess until recently; and in dealing with which you may experience some embarrassment. I, of course, allude to the negroes. Among the terms upon which the Confederate States terminated their heroic struggle for a separate and independent nationality, was one which guaranteed freedom to this race. Although we deplore that result, as alike injurious to the country and fatal to the negroes, the law has been placed upon our statute books in solemn form by us through our delegates. The laws for their government, as slaves, have been repealed and others substituted adapted to their new condition. We are in honor bound to observe these laws. For myself I do not hesitate to say in private and public, officially and unofficially, that, after doing all I could to avert it, when I took off my sword in surrender I determined to observe the terms of that surrender with the same earnestness and fidelity with which I first shouldered my musket. True manhood requires no deception, but that as we say with our lips we shall feel with our hearts, and do with our hands.

"There is nothing in the history of the past of which we need be ashamed. Whilst we cherish its glorious memories, and that of our martyred dead, we pause here and there to drop a tear over their consecrated ashes, but remember there is still work for the living, and set ourselves about the task of re-establishing society and rebuilding our ruined homes. Others unwilling to submit to this condition of things may seek their homes abroad. You and I are bound to this soil for life, for better or for worse, and it must at last cover our remains.

"What then is our duty? To repine at our lot? That is not the part of manliness; but to rise up, going forward, performing our highest missions as men. 'He who does the best his circumstances allow, does well—acts nobly; angels could do no more.' Is it not enough that the blood of the best and bravest has been shed in every battle throughout the land? Is it not enough that the bones of our fathers and brothers and sons lie whitening on every hill top? Is it not enough that the voice of lamentation has been heard at every fireside? Is it not enough that the wailings of the widows and orphans still sound in our ears? Have we not suffered enough? Have we not done all that was in the power of human nature? In our bosoms let us wear this consciousness as a jewel above price.

"Now let us deal with the facts before us as they are. The negro has been made free. It is no work of his. He did not seek freedom, and nominally free as he is, he is, beyond expression, helpless by his want of habits of self-reliance, helpless by his want of experience, and doubly helpless by his want of comprehension to understand and appreciate his condition. From the very nature of his surroundings, so far as promoting his welfare and adapting him to this new relation to society are concerned, all agencies from abroad must prove inadequate. They may restrain in individual instances, but we are the only people in the world who understand his character, and hence, the only people in the world capable of managing him.

"To remedy the evils growing out of the abolition of slavery it seems two things are necessary: First, a recognition of the freedom of the race as a fact, the enactment of just and humane laws, and the willing enforcement of them. Secondly, by treating them with perfect fairness and justice in our contracts, and in every way in which we may be brought in contact with them.

"By the first we convince the world of our good faith, and get rid of the system of espionage, by removing the pretext of its necessity; and by the second, we secure the services of the negroes, teach them their places, and how to keep them, and convince them at last that we are indeed their best friends. When we do this let us hope that society will revive from its present shock, and our land be crowned with abundant harvests. We need the labor of the negro all over the country, and it is worth the effort to secure it. If it would not be extending this charge beyond what I conceive to be a proper limit of time for its delivery, I might enlarge upon this subject by showing the depressing effect upon the country which would be produced by the sudden removal of so much of its productive labor. Its effect would be the decreased value of the lands, decreased agricultural products, decreased revenue to the State and country, arising from these sources, with their thousand attendant results.

"Besides all this, which appeals to our interests, gentlemen, do we owe the negro any grudge? What has he himself done to provoke our hostility? Shall we be angry with him because freedom has been forced upon him? Shall it excite our animosity because he has been suddenly and without any effort on his part, torn loose from the protection of a kind master? He is proud to call you Master yet. In the name of humanity let him do so. He may have been the companion of your boyhood. He may be older than you, and perhaps carried you in his arms when an infant. You may be bound to him by a thousand ties which only a Southern man knows, and which he alone can feel in all its force. It may be that when, only a few years ago, you girded on your cartridge-box and shouldered your trusty rifle, to go to meet the invaders of your country, you committed to his care your home and your loved ones; and when you were far away upon the weary march, upon the dreadful battle-field, in the trenches, and on the picket line, many and many a time you thought of that faithful old negro, and your heart warmed towards him."

This charge to the Grand Jury of Pike County shows somewhat the condition into which the country had been plunged by the termination of the war. "The brutalities of progress are called revolutions, but when they are ended the fact is recognized; the human race has been chastised, but it has moved onwards."

No one can realize the severe ordeal the Southern people were required to pass through during the process of Reconstruction but those of us who experienced it. Thousands of negroes, uneducated, unfitted for anything except to obey and to do their duty each day as directed by a superior, were given in one day their freedom; and not only that, but all the privileges of citizenship. Their conduct in this trying time should prove to the world the love, fear, and high regard which they entertained for their former masters. There is nothing I think in the records of the history of the world like their docility and willingness to be law-abiding citizens under these extraordinary circumstances. It would seem natural that so great and sudden a change in their condition would have proven too much for them, and that they would have become intoxicated, as it were. As it was, we could have managed them splendidly and without dissatisfaction or distrust on their part, had the so-called "carpet baggers" kept out of our midst. They, in many instances, used the negro for their own advancement by getting his vote, and procuring the offices of the State which should have been filled by our own reliable men.

We were not only subjected to these

political troubles, but we were bereft of our property without any compensation. The experience of my husband and myself was the experience of thousands. We were married early in life, and had applied ourselves closely to duty, and consequently saved some money each year. This money was invested to the best advantages the time afforded and in a way then legally sanctioned; viz., in slaves. From 1850 to 1865 we labored with the view of securing the wherewithal to educate our children (and God blessed us with a goodly number), and have something ready for the winter of old age. In 1865 we had all our earnings swept away; nothing remained except the consciousness of having done our duty "in that state of life unto which it had pleased God to call us."

I believe now, that Slavery is a detriment to any country, and if I could by any act of mine re-establish it here and get back my slaves, I would not do it. But the government of the United States has the credit of giving the black man his freedom, while it was at the expense of the Southern people; and we feel the loss.

We had to begin life over, as it were. The farm had been carried on with Joe as foreman, as in the days of Slavery, for two years, when Mr. Clayton thought best to make a change; and in the fall Joe came up to talk of the business for the next year.

My husband said:

"Joe, what shall we do?"

Joe replied, "Whatever you say, Marster."

Then my husband said, "Well, Joe, that is what you have said every time. Now I want to know what does Joe say."

He said, "Well, Master, I am tired worryin' wid dese free niggers, and would like to have a little farm of my own."

There was a house on an eighty-acre lot over on the far end of the plantation which my husband told him he would sell him, and let him pay so much each year until it was paid for. The house consisted of two large rooms and a hall. Joe and Nancy very soon were moved and fixed up with all that was necessary for a farm.

Thus I lost my good cook, and began my experience with the freedman as servant. I well remember my first effort at preparing a meal of substantial food. The making of delicacies, cakes and desserts of different kinds, I had learned when I had first begun life as a housekeeper; but to boil vegetables and prepare the common dishes were things the negroes all knew so well that they had been left to them for preparation.

Nancy had been my cook for so many years that she had learned to make beautiful light-bread and cakes, also to put up fruits of various kinds, jellies, wines, etc. Every Friday in my home bread was made for Sunday, that it might be a day of rest for all. Friday was selected for the baking, so if the cook did not succeed well there would be another day in which to work. Nancy adopted these rules in the management of her house. Her family consisted of Joe and herself and one little boy which she had taken during slavery. His mother died when he was only one year old, and Nancy asked if she might take the boy. We were glad to let her have the child, knowing she would take his mother's place.

Every Sunday morning Nancy would send me a basket of good things from her store room, something, she would say, to help out Missus's dinner, and it was always acceptable. She would often invite the whole of my family to come over and take dinner with her—my husband, myself, and my children comprising the family under the new order of things. I had so many children that I would hesitate to take them all to dine with a neighbor generally, but not with this good woman and friend. She esteemed it a great privilege to have "her white folks" spend the day with her. Her table was always covered with a beautiful white cloth, and plenty of silver, obtained by her at the agricultural fairs. Her dinners were all that an epicure could wish. She and "Sonny," as she called her boy, would wait on us while we were eating, and when we had finished our dinner and gone into the sitting room, her family would sit down and eat their dinner. They never for one moment thought of sitting down to the table with

"Master's" folks. We never went to her house but that she would have us eat something. They both toiled late and early and were blessed with plenty.

The negroes were, and are, proud to have lived with the better class of whites, but have always had a contempt for the poorer class. They would call them "poor Buckra."

My husband's brother had a man named Lewis, who, when a small boy, was a waiter at his father's home. I saw him there when we were married and made my first visit to his parents. A bright boy he was. After this brother's death, occasioned from a wound received at Murfreesboro, his property was divided and Lewis came into our possession. After Emancipation Lewis remained with us many years. His home was only a short distance from our home. He cultivated a farm successfully, and soon had acquired not only the necessaries of life, but some luxuries. He had a pair of nice horses, a buggy and wagon, and other things, and lived well; but he had never known freedom entirely without Mars' Henry's supervision.

One day he came to the conclusion that he would move away and enjoy freedom to its fullest extent. He came to see Mr. Clayton in the fall to say something about it. He seemed embarrassed when Mr. Clayton addressed him:

"Lewis, what is it you want?"

"Well, Mars' Henry, I want to move away and feel ontirely free and see whut I cen do by mysef. You has been kind to me and I has done well, but I want to go anyhow."

Mr. Clayton said, "Very well, Lewis, that is all right, move when you please; but when you leave, nail up the door of your house and leave it until you want to come back. No one else shall go into it."

Lewis and his brother, Ned, rented a farm some miles beyond Clayton, moved, and we heard no more of them until the next fall, when Lewis made his appearance, very much dejected.

Mr. Clayton said, "How are you, Lewis? How are you getting on?"

"Bad, Mars' Henry. I have come to ask ef I cen go into my old house again."

Lewis and Ned had hired hands, gotten a merchant to furnish them, and lost almost everything they had started out with. Lewis moved back, and has been loath to leave the Claytons since, and is now with us, an old man. Ned died very soon after with pneumonia. His wife, Betsey, soon followed him to the grave. She had consumption, something almost unheard of with the colored people when slavery existed, but which is now a common disorder with them.

In 1874 Gen. Clayton came out as a candidate for the office of Circuit Judge, his disabilities having been removed. He said to me one Saturday, "Victoria, I must start out on Monday to see the people of this Judicial Circuit, and I do dislike so much to go alone, and wish you could go with me."

"Well," I said, "send for my sister to take care of the children and my household generally, and I will take the baby and go with you." The baby was only six months old—our Benjamin, the last of the generous number God had given us. My sister was brought, and on Monday morning we started in a buggy, railroads being unknown in these southeastern counties of Alabama.

We traveled from one little town to another, meeting many friends, and kindness on every hand.

I remember one instance particularly. A Mr. Godwin and his wife, who lived in one of these little towns, had come to Clayton several years before to sell their small crop and buy some supplies. Mr. Clayton met them and insisted on their coming to our home to spend the night, instead of camping as they intended doing. They came. They were good, plain, country people. We treated them with the greatest courtesy and attention possible, and next morning when they were ready to leave, I had a nice lunch prepared for their enjoyment on their way home. They always remembered this visit to our house with pleasure. In our travels we drove up to their home one evening about twilight. The old man was standing near the gate at the time, and as soon as he discovered who we were, he called in a loud tone of voice for his wife to come and see who had come.

She came out quickly to see. She was a large, strong-looking woman, and just lifted me and my baby in her embrace. The little fellow did not know what was the matter. So loud and close a demonstration frightened him terribly; but after some little time, peace was restored, and we were domiciled for the night.

The next morning, at a very early hour, the people could be seen coming from the surrounding country, some on foot, some in buggies, some on horseback, and many in wagons, sitting in chairs, and many a well filled basket was brought. They came in to hear Mr. Clayton make a speech. After the speaking, which was under the forest trees, the baskets were opened and a bountiful dinner spread for all.

This electioneering jaunt was very much enjoyed by us. It carried us back to our early married life. All care being left behind, we felt young again.

Mr. Clayton was elected to the office, which he filled many years, and made a considerable reputation as a Judge. The colored population looked upon him as their special friend. They would often be heard to say, "I know the Jedge will see thet I hev jestice." In dealing with these people he always remembered the few opportunities they had had to fit themselves for the responsibilities of citizenship, and extended to them all the leniency the law would permit. He endeavored "to do justly and love mercy."

The salary of the Judge's office being very small, we were forced to practise economy in every way we could, to provide for our very large family. By this time our former slaves were scattered far and wide, but we always had some near enough to claim our sympathy in sickness and sorrow. Times had changed, oh, so much! One can hardly realize how much, and in so short a time.

Old Joe, after some years of prosperity, was stricken with disease. Nancy sent over to me to send her a blue mass pill; that Joe was sick. The medicine was sent, and next morning I called one of my little boys to go with me to see how Uncle Joe was, and to take him some delicacies.

We walked over the fields to his house and found him very critically ill. I said to him:

"Joe, you must have a doctor."

He answered in a feeble voice, "Mistus, I trust in Jesus."

I said to him, "Having a doctor will not show a want of your trust in your Saviour."

He hesitated, and I made this illustration to him:

"Does not God cause the wheat and corn to grow to be made into bread to sustain man?"

"Yes, ma'am," he replied.

"Well, don't you have to plant the grain, cultivate it, and then have it ground to make the bread? And you believe this is right?"

"Yes, ma'am."

"Then why not use the medicine that God has filled the earth with, prepared by those who have studied what each herb is good for? Doctors have made it their business to learn how to prepare and give these medicines, a gift from God to His creatures."

Old Joe then said, "Mistus, send for the doctor."

The doctor was called in immediately, but when he came he told me that the chances were against him.

That night Judge Clayton came home on his way from one Court to another.

He indulged in a needed rest after his long day's drive, then went over to see his faithful and beloved old friend, and sat by him during the lonely watches of the night. The next morning he resumed his journey towards duty, but not until instructions had been given for a respectable burial of Joe, as he knew Joe would never get up again. He lived but a few hours. And now, in sight of the little cottage where this faithful old man spent the sunset of his life, there lies a lonely grave with the solemn pine trees above it forever singing a requiem for his soul that has gone

"To that fair land, upon whose strand
No wind of winter moans."

After Joe's death, Nancy got on very well, as her boy, Sonny, had grown to be almost a man, and could partially fill Joe's place. They lived very happily for many years, when this boy, in an evil hour, gathered up all the money she had and left her. She came over in great distress to get Master to make Sonny come back, not doubting Master's ability to do anything he wished. Mr. Clayton told her that Sonny was of age and she could not compel him to come back.

Sonny returned in penitence the next year. Nancy was very ambitious to live well and have many things around her, consequently she over-estimated her strength, and in a few years became a victim to a lingering disease. During this time we visited her constantly and loved to minister to her wants, temporally and spiritually, and with the assistance of my Prayer Book I believe I gave her comfort in these days of gloom. She died, and we were constrained to feel that another friend had left us.

Thus passed away two noble people. Though their skins were black, their souls were as pure and white as the driven snow. Earth has rarely had better, and few like them.

VIII.

BECOMING A SLAVEHOLDER AGAIN.

JACK, another of our old servants, came to me some years after his freedom, and wanted me to take one of his children, a boy of seven years of age. His wife had died, and the boy, Charley, was quite delicate, and he wanted some one to take care of him.

I said, "Jack, give him to me, and I will do the best in my power to raise him right, and make him a useful man."

In a few days after, it being Christmas morning, Jack came in and said:

"Miss Vicky, here is Charley."

The writings of trust were signed by

Becoming a Slaveholder Again.

him, and Charley has been my property ever since. He has grown to be a man in height and almost in years. He is a good, obedient boy, and really has become quite an institution in my family. One of my daughters undertook to educate him, and tried every evening for a whole winter to teach him, and at the end of the winter he did not know all of the alphabet, so she gave up his education in disgust. Then another daughter began the task, and, after much trouble and patience, got him through the first reader. He is a bright boy, except in "book learning." He can count money, tell the time by the clock or a watch, and do an errand as intelligently as any boy. His father has been opposed to his being taught to read and write, because he says if he learns to write he will be in the penitentiary for some meanness, and Charley himself said:

"Miss Mary, God did not make niggers to learn books."

And it is true, many of the young boys that have grown up since the war have been sent to the penitentiary for obtaining money by the means of knowing how to write.

Mr. Hilliard, in a book recently published, says:

"To-day not a slave treads the soil of freedom, from the waters of the St. Lawrence to the Mexican sea, from the shore of the Atlantic, where the rising sun greets the Flag of the Republic, to the distant coast of the Pacific, where his setting beams kindly upon its fold."

I would like to show him Charley and tell him he is mistaken. Charley is bound by law to me, and is as much under my control as one of my own children. And here again Scripture comes in—see Gal. iv.

Charley is almost like one of my children. When he arrives at his majority he may leave me to find out how absolute freedom feels. Now he is as submissive as one of my old slaves, and as much attached to the family.

A short time before the war we bought a woman with two children who had been brought from Maryland, and as soon as she knew she was free, she said to Mr. Clayton:

"Master, I want to save up my wages to go back to my old home."

So at the end of the year he would give her his note calling for the amount due her. At the end of the second year she concluded to return. Being a woman of very little sense, Mr. Clayton was afraid to have her start off in the usual way to reach Washington, whither she wanted to go; so he bought her passage through the Express, and the balance of her money which she had accumulated she put into her bosom. Thus she and her children left Eufaula, with a well filled basket of lunch for the trip. Mr. Clayton wrote to a gentleman in Washington to meet her and help her arrange her matters on her arrival, which he did. When members of the family visit the city they frequently see Jane. She comes to inquire about her friends down South.

These instances and facts concerning our old slaves I mention to show the love and trust that existed between the master and his slave in our Southern land. As I have said before, many of us thought Slavery a curse to our land. Yet what were we to do but to make the best of existing laws and environments?

My husband became tired of the onerous duties of his Judicial office, after fourteen years of constant labor, and, the salary being so small a compensation, he decided to make a change, and the Presidency of the University of Alabama was tendered him. He resigned the Judgeship and accepted this new position.

It was a hard trial to gather up and leave our dear old home. Every tree and flower were dear to us. There our children had been born. There we had seen many of them grow up to manhood and womanhood. There we had spent many happy years. In the little town, we had by hard work built a little church to the glory of God, and in our home stood the prophet's room always ready for him when he made his regular visitations.

BISHOP COBBS.

And then the dear, sainted Bishop Cobbs had rested under our roof each year when he made his annual visit to this corner of his vineyard, and since his death

BISHOP WILMER

the beloved Bishop Wilmer has done the same. All these remembrances endeared the home to us.

"There is a land of every land the pride,
Beloved by Heaven o'er all the world beside;
Where shall that land, that spot of earth be found?
Art thou a man? a patriot? look around;
Oh! thou shalt find, howe'er thy footsteps roam,
That land thy country, that spot thy home."

Lewis, the man who had lived with us all these years, came to ask the privilege of going with us. He said:

"Mars' Henry, are you goin' to Tuscaloosa?"

"Yes."

"Well, let me go with you? Wherever you go, I want to go too."

He felt like Ruth when she said to Naomi, "Whither thou goest, I will go; and where thou lodgest, I will lodge; thy people shall be my people, and thy God my God."

Lewis, with one other of our old

President's Mansion,
University of Alabama, Tuscaloosa.

slaves, went with us to our new home. Our family of children numbered only five then, three boys and two girls; our other children having made homes for themselves.

After we had been in Tuscaloosa a few months, one night some one knocked at the door, and on opening it to see who it was, some one said, "Mars' Henry, I have come to cook for you."

We found it was our old cook whom we had left behind in Clayton.

The last night we spent in our old home, the young people of the town came out with instruments of music to bid farewell to the old house where they had spent so many happy evenings. How sad the farewell was to me! On the next morning, the 13th day of August, 1886, there was a marriage in the dear little church very early, which we attended; then we boarded the train on our way to the untried life that awaited us in Tuscaloosa.

In Tuscaloosa everything was different from our mode of living on a farm. Gen. Clayton put all his earnestness and zeal into his work for the State, trying to mould her young sons to fill creditably the important places they would soon be called upon to fill. Here he labored for three years, and made many strong friends, particularly among the fathers of these young men committed to his care.

In the beginning of the fourth scholastic year, early in October, he came home from his office one day about eleven o'clock. This being an unusual hour for his return, I went to meet him, and asked him what was the matter. He said:

"Victoria, I am sick."

With my assistance, he was soon in bed. He said:

"Call me a little before 2 o'clock, as I am to lecture then to the Law class."

I sat down by the bedside to watch with anxious care as only a loving wife can; but before the time had expired, he arose, drank a cup of tea, and went over to the University to deliver his lecture to the Law class.

When he returned after the close of his duties for the day, he said that the cup of tea refreshed him very much, and that he spent a very interesting hour with the students, and really enjoyed it. Little did we think it was the last hour he would spend with these young men.

The next day he felt better, and attended to his usual duties; but that night he became worse, and the next morning we had the surgeon come to see him.

The doctor did not think anything serious the matter, and gave him some simple medicine. Several hours later he fainted and never rallied. Another physician was called in, but they could do nothing for his relief. On the 13th of October his spirit was taken to the God who gave it, and we were left to mourn the loss; not only a loss to his sorrowing family, but a loss to the State of Alabama, which he had served so faithfully, through every vicissitude.

The colored people considered it a special loss to them, as he had always shown to them justice and kindness—"rich in love and sweet humanity."

The Trustees of the University requested me to remain in the President's home until the expiration of the scholastic year, which I did.

One of my daughters married Dr. Rogers, of Memphis, Tenn., and with my other four children I moved to Eufaula. Lewis and Charley, our colored friends, form a part of my household until the present time.

Here ends my simple story, which I trust may help to show some of our Northern brethren the good there was in the institution of Slavery as it existed in the Southern States; and may engender a more just judgment of the white man who lived under the Old Regime in the South.

I hope also that it may arouse pleasant memories in the minds of old friends, and may prove of interest to my children and their descendants, as well as give them correct impressions of the inner life of a Christian slave-holding household; and an idea also of the life and purposes of the first Confederate Colonel.